GENERAL CROOK AND THE APACHE WARS

BY CHARLES R. LUMMIS

EDITED BY TURBESÉ LUMMIS FISKE

FOREWORD BY DUDLEY GORDON

ILLUSTRATIONS BY DON PERCEVAL

NORTHLAND PRESS

FLAGSTAFF, ARIZONA

FIRST EDITION

Second Printing, 1985

ISBN 0-87358-387-6

Library of Congress Catalog Card No. 65-17580

COMPOSED AND PRINTED IN THE UNITED STATES OF AMERICA

FOREWORD

THE GENERAL to whom Geronimo surrendered, and whose campaign tactic of pursue — pursue — pursue brought the Apache wars to an end, never received proper credit for his well-earned achievement.

Brigadier General George Crook was seasoned by thirty-three years of successful Civil War and Indian campaigns when Geronimo, Chihuahua and other Apache warleaders again crossed the Mexican border into Arizona and committed numerous horrible depredations on ranchers, miners, and traveling immigrants. General Crook pursued the Apaches so relentlessly that on March 25, 1886, Geronimo requested a conference to discuss terms of surrender.

By that time General Crook had distinguished himself in Indian fighting. Among his many credits were his crushing defeat of the strong Apache nation in 1873 when five thousand hostiles surrendered to him at Camp Verde; and when he out-generaled and routed more than four thousand Sioux and their Cheyenne and Arapahoe allies only one week after they had annihilated Custer and his whole command in 1877. With the surrender of Geronimo, he should have terminated fifteen years of unspeakable and costly depredations by the fierce renegade Apaches, were it not for a greedy white trader.

General Crook had returned from his duties among the Sioux to the Department of Arizona, September 4, 1882. From then until March, 1883, all was quiet among the Apaches. Crook used the interval to train his scouts and to show the Indians on the reservation the advantages of being civilized and self-sustaining. He gave them the opportunity for self-government.

As he had foreseen, the renegades in Mexico under Geronimo, Chatto, Chihuahua, etc., who had been chafing from inactivity in the mountains, set out on a series of raiding parties in Arizona and New Mexico, then retreated across the border. The General, having received authorization from Washington, made every possible preparation and set out in pursuit "regardless of national lines" on May 1, 1883.

General Crook, aided by Pe-nal-tishu (Peaches), who had deserted from the hostiles, was able to trail the renegades into the depths of their hitherto impregnable stronghold in the rugged Sierra Madre mountains in Sonora, Mexico. Soon, after several hot engagements, the weary Apache leaders, knowing General Crook's skill as a soldier, and having confidence in him as a man of honor, decided to give up.

The outcome was that Geronimo, Chihuahua, Chatto, Bonito, Loco and Keowtennay said to General Crook: "We give ourselves up. Do with us as you please." Crook took them at their word and, without disarming them, he brought every one of the five hundred renegades to the reservation. At the time he had two hundred and forty men under him.

For the next two years there was not an outrage or depredation of any kind committed by an Apache. Then came the outbreak of a hundred and thirty-four Apaches, ninety-two of them women and children, on May 17, 1885.

After ten months of wearying pursuit, the renegades once more retreated to the Sierra Madres. Here again, through the aid of the scout Peaches, General Crook caught up with them, and here again they sent word saying they wanted to talk about giving up.

Upon receiving the request for a conference, General Crook agreed to meet the chiefs in the Cañon de Los Embudos, twenty-five miles below the Mexican border, on March 25, 1886.

The terms offered by General Crook were simple and direct: complete surrender and their lives, or continued pursuit until every renegade was killed. After a three-day palaver, Geronimo and the war chiefs Chihuahua, Kut-le, Natchez and Nanay agreed to an unconditional surrender, March 27, 1886.

His mission having been accomplished, General Crook set out for Fort Bowie, Arizona, to communicate by telegraph to the War Department. He left the seventy-seven captives to be conducted to the fort by Lieutenant Marion P. Maus and his battalion of a hundred scouts.

On March 29, after two days of marching, the prisoners camped near the border at Smuggler's Springs where the notorious Tribolet succeeded in supplying Geronimo and a few of his followers with base lies regarding the treatment they might expect — and several demijohns of liquid courage. By daylight the next morning Geronimo and Natchez and some thirty followers had fled into almost impassable mountains.

When word that the Apaches had surrendered was flashed over the wires the country was elated. The then Colonel Harrison G. Otis, publisher of the *Los Angeles Times* and an old-time campaigner with General Crook, sent Charles F. Lummis into the field to cover the story. When Lummis arrived at Fort Bowie on March 31 he learned that Geronimo and Natchez and their followers had spooked and escaped, leaving Chihuahua, Kut-le, Ulzanna and old Nanay and their followers. He remained on the scene nearly three months.

Also, upon his arrival Lummis discovered that he was the only press representative in the area. No others had been there. The scare headlines which alarmed the readers of papers all over the country were the result of Associated Press reports derived from second-, third- and fourth-hand distortions of the facts.

Few people since Kit Carson have known the terrain of Arizona as intimately as author-editor-historian Charles Lummis. Carson knew it chiefly from the saddle of a pony; Lummis knew it from having hiked through it from Manuelito to Needles — how could one know it more intimately! With a side trip to the Grand Canyon, that made over five hundred miles of intimacy at thirty miles per day. This occurred in 1884/85 when he walked from Cincinnati to Los Angeles where he became City Editor of the *Los*

Angeles Times the day following his arrival. Along the route he had written characteristically vigorous accounts describing his observations and adventures. These weekly letters he had forwarded to the *Times*. When he arrived in the City of the Angels in February, 1885, he learned that they had doubled the circulation of the paper.

Prior to hiking to Los Angeles, Lummis, New England born and Harvard trained, had worked for two years as Editor of the *Scioto Gazette* in Chillicothe, Ohio. When he began his duties in Los Angeles, the city was in the midst of its period of greatest expansion during the boom of the eighties which followed the completion of the Southern Pacific and the Santa Fe railroads, which made Los Angeles a transcontinental terminus. Health seekers and investors came faster than housing could be provided, the buying of property was at a fever pitch, and of course the *Times* prospered.

When news of Geronimo's (false alarm) surrender was released, publisher Otis sent Lummis into the field for first-hand accounts of on-the-scene news regarding the imprisonment and disposal of the renegade Apaches whose atrocities had horrified readers over the country.

During the months following his arrival at the scene of action, Lummis, employing the flamboyant and sometimes grandiloquent style of space writers of the day, reported to the rapidly increasing number of *Times* readers on the physical aspects of the war area, the characteristics and war practices of the crafty Apache, the manner of man General Crook was, and the nature of the opposition to him in the press and among the politicians and merchants who profited from the "disturbance." He also revealed the difficulties faced by General Crook in tracking down the enemy and the various reactions by the citizenry of the time. A news item in the *Silver City Enterprise* (New Mexico) dated December 23, 1886, reveals in what fear Geronimo was held. It reads:

"CITIZENS MEETING

Yesterday afternoon a citizen's meeting was called to devise means for immediate relief from the present Indian troubles. As an initiative step it was moved that a meeting of the Grant County stock association be called. . . . A motion was put and carried that the board of county commissioners be requested to offer a reward of $250 for the scalps of marauding Indians. To this amount Lyons and Campbell offered an additional award of $500 for Geronimo's scalp."

Although Geronimo typified all that was horrendous in the Apache, he was not a chief. He was a medicine man and prophet. He was outranked by several others in his tribe, but he was undoubtedly the leader of the small group of renegades, thirty-four men and women, who escaped into the Sierra Madre mountains and eluded the pursuit of General Miles, Crook's successor, for nearly three months.

As a prophet, Geronimo wielded a superstitious power which civilized man cannot comprehend. Often he foretold events with accuracy which time and distance should have prevented. A case in point, one among several, appears in *I Fought With Geronimo*, by Jason Betzinez, on page 115:

"During the council that evening Geronimo made another prophecy: 'Tomorrow afternoon as we march along the north side of the mountains we will see a man standing on a hill to our left. He will howl to us and tell us that the troops have captured our base camp.'

We marched quite early the next morning, straight west through a wide forest of oaks and pines. About the middle of the afternoon we heard a howl from the hilltop to our left. There stood an Apache calling to us. He came down through the rocks to tell us that the main camp, now some fifteen miles distant, was in the hands of U. S. troops. General Crook with some cavalry and Indian scouts had taken all the rest of the Apaches into custody.

Thus the event which Geronimo had foretold when we were still several days' journey away, and had repeated last night, came to pass as true as steel. I still cannot explain it."

Lummis was no apologist for the butchery of Geronimo, but as a historian he had to give credit where credit was due. As a poet, Lummis later felt moved to write a thirty-two-stanza epic poem commemorating the signal military achievement of Geronimo, leading twenty bucks — and living off army supplies — while he avoided the U.S. Army for months. Two stanzas follow:

> They never saw a hair of him,
>   but ever and oft they felt —
> Each rock and cactus spitting lead
>   from an Apache belt,
> Where never sign of man there was,
>   nor flicker of a gun —
> You cannot fight an empty hill;
>   you run — if left to run!
> A Prophet of his people, he,
>   no War Chief, but their priest,
> And strong he made his Medicine,
>   and deep the mark he creased —

The most consummate Warrior
since warfare first began,
The deadliest Fighting Handful
in the calendar of Man.

Most readers have been led to believe that the Apaches were rebellious from pure "orneriness." Actually, a white man, the Indian Agent at the San Carlos Reservation, was largely responsible for that orneriness. In fact, most of the Apache outbreaks and the resulting depredations came as a reaction to the mistreatment experienced by the Indians at the hands of the Indian Agents.

The report of the Federal Grand Jury of the Territory of Arizona of October, 1882, supports this point. Now federal grand juries of the frontier were not notably sympathetic to Indians, but this jury went on record to say that:

The Indian Agent at the San Carlos Reservation was a disgrace to the civilization of the age, a foul blot upon the national escutcheon. . . . [We] express our utter abhorrence of the conduct of that class of reverend peculators who have cursed Arizona as Indian officials and who have caused more misery and loss of life than all other causes combined. . . . [and practiced] fraud and villainy constantly . . . in open violation of laws and in defiance of public justice. Fraud, peculation, conspiracy, larceny. . . . With the immense power wielded by the Indian Agent, almost any crime is possible. . . . Meantime, the Indians are neglected, half-fed, discontented and turbulent. . . . To these and kindred causes may be attributed the desolation and bloodshed that have dotted our plains with the graves of murdered victims.

But many citizens were equally dissatisfied with Crook's

record of dealing with the Apaches. Two fairly typical expressions of ire appeared in the *Silver City Enterprise*. They are characteristic of the attitude of the press throughout the territories. Under dateline of Deming, New Mexico, June 13, 1885, one E. B. L. wrote:

As Geronimo has acquired a national reputation, a sketch of his history will be of interest, while it will also illustrate the government Indian policy as carried out by that terrific Indian fighter Gen. Crook. . . . Here in the same year that phenomenal Indian fighter, Gen. Crook, paid Geronimo a visit, accompanied by U.S. troops and about 300 Indian scouts. He did not capture the renegades, but after a parley returned to U.S. soil. During the last twelve years Crook's Apache friends have butchered in cold blood. . . . The General's great hobby is his Apache scouts with which he expects to run down the renegades. Who are these scouts? Why they are mostly Apache Indians, friends and relatives of Geronimo's band. . . . This scouting is simply a training-school for hostile leaders. . . . If it gets too hot for the renegades, they can surrender and are assured good treatment. . . . In reality, the Indians are about the ugliest and filthiest brutes on the globe — lying, thieving, gambling cut-throats, [who,] when a beef is cut up and distributed among them, will quarrel over the entrails, and eat the filthy stuff raw or half-cooked. . . .

And in conclusion:

The citizens of these territories are at last thoroughly aroused. Our local press without exception are publishing the storm of indignation against Crook and the war department, and every paper contains offers of prominent citizens to arm and furnish men to exterminate the occupants of the reservation (6,000), be they good or bad. The government has been appealed to year after year to stop this annual butchery, but the war department, on the strength of the representations of such Indian-fighters as Pope, Crook and Hatch, pigeon-hole the whole business, and wonder why the frontier folk are kicking up such a fuss over nothing! Haven't they got the army to attend to the Indians?

What the citizens demand is: That the scouts be discharged; that every hostile found off the reservation and captured shall be turned over to the civil authorities; that the Indians at San Carlos be completely disarmed, or that the reservation be abandoned. If not, the San Carlos reservation will be raided and thousands of good Indians made.

E. B. L.

And from Hillsboro, New Mexico, November 4, 1885, came the following:

In your issue of Oct. 30 is an article by "L". He asks "Where are the men who some months ago were offering to subscribe hundreds of dollars to outfit a force to raid the reservation? Their ardor seems to have cooled until next spring's outbreak again revives it."

I submitted a proposition to the citizens of Grand and Sierra counties. I saw no other. Mine is still submitted, and if "L" and eight of his friends will "ante" I will meet them in Silver City.

I will give "L" $500 if he will deliver Geronimo dead or alive, at Silver City, N. M. I had no "ardor" in the permises [sic]. I asserted a business proposition to accomplish a certain object. . . .

With "L" I think the reservation should be raided. — K.K.K. them. — H. W. Elliott

xiv

Lummis, however, was impressed with Crook. He wrote, "There is something about the General which makes one want to take one's hat off in his presence." And of the words General Crook said about Indians, Lummis kept them in mind when, a few years later, he founded the Sequoyah League whose aim was "To Make Better Indians by Treating Them Better." His goal was to make first class Indians of them, instead of second class Americans.

By the time General Nelson A. Miles, the replacement for General Crook, arrived at Fort Bowie on April 11, 1886, Crook had already captured and returned to the reservation three-quarters of the hostiles who had broken out in May of the year before, including four war chiefs. Only Geronimo and Natchez and thirty-two fugitives, weary from ten months of persistent pursuit, remained to be taken.

Miles placed Captain Henry W. Lawton, later General Lawton, assisted by Lieutenant Charles B. Gatewood, in command of the scouts in July and, acting upon a rumor that Geronimo was just below the Mexican border and tiring from being pursued, Lawton and Gatewood headed south with troops and scouts. In August the hostiles were spotted on Tall Mountain. Here scouts Kay-i-tah and Martine volunteered to carry, under a flag of truce, General Miles' message demanding the surrender of Geronimo and his party, without guarantees.

After some haggling, Geronimo surrendered to Lieutenant Gatewood who accepted in the name of General Miles, then Gatewood conducted the captives to Captain Lawton's camp. Lawton offered Geronimo the same terms General Wood had offered him back in March — the Indians would keep their arms and would march back to Fort Bowie. Geronimo agreed. Captain Lawton immediately sent a messenger to Fort Bowie requesting General Miles to meet the marching party on the way to the fort and to accept Geronimo's surrender. This the General did.

Meanwhile, with the people of Arizona howling for a hanging, President Cleveland had been vacillating from a parley policy to one of shoot-to-kill and back to parley again. By the time the party reached Fort Bowie, the order was to try the offenders for murder. This was most embarrassing to Captain Lawton who had already given his word to Geronimo. However, General Miles defied the presidential order and backed up Lawton.

In time the thirty-four Apaches were returned to the reservation, later transfered from there to Florida and then to Fort Sill, Oklahoma — and the Geronimo campaign was over.

Dudley Gordon

PREFACE

IN MY CHILDHOOD my father talked to me about many things, but he never told me about his months with General Crook, Nanay, Geronimo and the others of the Apache campaign. By the time I came along he had had many other adventures and his mind was full of more recent expeditions. But I grew up among trophies of that manhunt. Even when I was small I would peer into his precious curio cabinet at the heavy silver bracelets, the bloodstained headdress, the lanky Apache leggins with the shielded toe, and I would ponder about them and the necklace with the twofold crescent and the cross that sprang from a heart.

It is likely that my father never saw an Indian (outside

of a cartoon) before he was twenty-five. Like many native New Englanders, if he thought of the "red man" at all it was as an alien and a "savage." The Far West as a whole was only a little less out of the guidelines of blessed conformity. Surely such life as was to be found more than a thousand miles west of Harvard could have nothing much in common with *us*. And then he was precipitated into the most ego-shrinking and skull-stretching postgraduates course a strictly reared Methodist minister's son could have encountered. It was his Tramp Across the Continent.

"Why is it," he wrote long after, "that the last and most difficult education seems to be the ridding ourselves of ther silly inborn race prejudice? . . . And yet . . . men everywhere . . . are all just about the same thing. The difference is little deeper than the skin." During his journey he had trudged into the pueblo of San Ildefonso, New Mexico, unshaven and suspicious. He came out of it the friend and defender of the First American. He never forgot how thoses gentle brown brothers welcomed him to their homes as though this unknown tramp were their very own. A few weeks later in Arizona my father met the kind of "American" who helped to create the so-called Indian treacheries and to stir up vengeance and bloodshed only because they fattened his own pocket.

Early the following spring, my father was at work at his editorial desk when news of the fresh outbreak among the Apaches reached the offices of the *Los Angeles Times*. Nothing could have suited him more than to have Colonel Otis send him to write correspondence from the thick of the troubles. The Apache warrior was of another breed from the peaceful Pueblos of New Mexico, but my father found the "Turkey Mountain People" equally a part of the human race.

xviii

How much of a hold those brief days retained on his mind we glimpsed at the very end of his life. When he knew that he had but a few months to live, he chose, as one of the tasks he most wanted to do, to write that stinging ballad, "Man-Who-Yawns," about Geronimo. In it I began to see what those experiences had meant to my father. Yet it was not until he had gone from us to explore that farther frontier that I really commenced to appreciate how deep they had reached. It was the scrapbooks and photograph albums he left us that told me.

In their pictures and writings I began tracking down, almost like one of his Apache scouts, that Lummis I had never known. Here he appeared as a motherless boy with wistful rebellious face, there as a headlong experimenter with college duel and poison, then an unlikely young man with a beard like a budding Abraham — the picture that helped stop a bullet several years later. The picture of a sombreroed westerner on a bucking bronco was followed by other versions of Lummis till at last I came to those of the man we really knew. The strong fellow in white jeans hustling boulders in his arms to build a castle is our Lummis father; so is the portrait of the eagle-faced man Indians once had named "The Man Who Cares."

But also there is the portrait of the dark Apache, the menacing warrior with his hand on a dagger — nobody's idea of a blue-eyed Yankee, let alone a minister's son. Yet it was as a Chiricahua with long black hair and an Apache scowl that father had himself pictured to remind him of the fun and the color he enjoyed in the spring months of 1886. Now in the pages that follow you too may share, through my father's own words, the excitement of that spring.

Turbesé Lummis Fiske

xix

The following selected dispatches
originally appeared in the *Los Angeles
Times* during April and May, 1886.

CHAPTER

THERE IS AN OLD TRADITION in Arizona that "he who drinks the waters of the Hassayampa must return to drink again, and can never more tell the truth." As for the first part, I have no evidence, but I can testify as to the accuracy of the second.

The California liar has amassed notoriety not his own. He does well for his gifts, but he is overmatched. The boss, the unapproachable and supreme twister of truth's caudal appendage is the fiery, untamed, mouthful Arizonan — the multitudinous gentleman who has been feeding the Associated Press with reports of the Apache campaigns. Of these reports I believe it is moderate to say that not one in

fifteen has been even approximately true. Most of this economizer of the truth dwells in Tombstone — and by what scratch did Tombstone ever carom on the frigid facts? Part of him hangs out in Tucson — that arid aggregation of toughness, adobe and spare time, where people have too much leisure to tell the truth. He has some members-at-large in other parts of the territory. And when he unbuttons his mouth, it shall be a pity if you don't get some news.

Mayhap it is an errant "cow-puncher" who lopes into Tombstone, fills his hide with intestine corroder, and begins to shoot off his war news. That he has not been within fifty miles of the field does not bother him. He can tell you more about it in a day than Crook ever dared to know. "Bar-keep" takes it all in and retails it to the next customer, who pours it into the elastic receptivity of the Associated Press agent, who thereupon toots it to the gaping world. Or, perchance, it is some mule persuader discharged from the military pack train, who turns himself loose on the first unprotected settlement he strikes. Yet, again, it is the gentle tin-horn gambler who cajoles his hours of ease by putting up a cold deck on unsophisticated Truth and dealing a pat hand to the agent of the great news dispenser.

These are not guesses, but plain statements of the way in which the "news" for which we pay is born. I have in my hand at this moment specific clippings from just such sources, whooped up all over the country as the latest news. Now I don't argue that it is impossible for a drunken cowboy, deposed burro-beater or tin-cornucopia professor to stumble some time upon the truth. Accidents will happen. Nor do I know that the Associated Press is to blame. Like all the rest of us it has been imposed upon. Aside, however, from the merely unreliable sources from which the news has been drawn, there is a strong anti-Crook ring, of unknown periphery, of many diverse materials, of great evident weight, homologous only in the desire to "down Crook." It is not surprising, therefore, to find that the Territorial papers have been abominably abused in the matter of war news from this section. Until now no newspaper has had a representative anywhere near the field. The Associated Press has had no agent within one hundred miles of the fighting, nor has it sent any person even to headquarters for news. No dispatches have been sent out from anywhere by any actually posted person, until the arrival of your correspondent.

To begin with, no man can grip the full breadth of the situation who does not know this Arizona country root and branch, and none can get even a finger in Truth's pie who has not a fair realization of the following physical facts. No campaign either in the Civil War nor any of the northern Indian wars was ever so entangled and crippled by topographical cussedness. Apachedom is a desert, partially redeemable, it is true, by the future development of artesian waters and canal irrigation, and already (in 1886) dotted with semi-occasional oases. But I can lead you five hundred miles, in a not palpably circuitous route, and in all that hideous stretch you will not see one drop of water, save the precious fluid in your water-kegs. This arid desert is not one vast sea of drifting sand. It is one of the most mountainous sections of the whole country. You will find square miles of it carpeted with the Etruscan gold of poppies and other miles of many another flower. The gray sagebrush, the greasewood's glaucous green, the emerald daggers of amole, the duller-hued bayonets of the aloe, topped with a banner of snowy bloom — these diversify all its valleys, while here and there loom the vast candelabras of giant cactus. Yet while all this is aesthetic it is not filling to those of us who must campaign there. Ride twenty miles across the flowery plain, and you would swap your tongue for a sun-baked sponge. Ride fifty without water and you will do well, indeed, if you ever see sanity again.

Then the mountains. Fancy an irregularly undulating but regularly thirsty plain of three hundred miles, broken by but three or four subterranean water-courses — a country from which, sans water, a bunk in Sheol would be a positive relief. Upon this vast area a wilderness of countless peaks and ridges, planted haphazard. Hunt the world over and you will find no more inhospitable and savage mountains. Shaggy with sharp rocks and sharper cactus, they rise five hundred to as many thousand feet above the circumfluent plain, their highest peaks wooded and snow-bound. You shall pass within a mile of such a hill and have no more notion of its inaccessibility than a cow has of the Hereafter. Try to climb the smallest and you will find out. There have never been but two animals which loomed up as successes in scaling these rocks — the mountain sheep and the Apache. These ranges form an "underground rail-way" over which a man of ordinary secretiveness could slink from Colorado to Mexico and never be seen by human eye. None but the high-circling buzzard and the prowling coyote would note his passing. Skulking through the mountains by day, dashing across the valleys by night, he could be as unobserved as if he burrowed underground. And even should some casual hostile glance detect him, he has but to shin up yonder crest and be safe. Himself almost absolutely unexposed, he can kill five hundred men as fast as they can come to him. And then he can sneak back from sheltering rock to rock until he is beyond pursuit. This is of course on the supposition that his foes are whites. He couldn't play that on the Apache. If a man who really hankered to hide out here got caught or killed, it would be because he was either a fool or playing to very hard luck.

That's the breed of topography they raise out here. And yet there are acres of good, rational people all over this country who fancy that all there is to this Apache business is to chase Lo over a field until he gets tired and then perforate him with a 45-70, or tie him up and bring him into camp in an express.

6

Now for the natur' of the native. Trying to hit the bull's eye of this matter at my limited verbal range is like trying to lasso a bronco steer with a piece of sewing-cotton. Hold the dictionary up by the tail, and still I can't shake out the vocabulary to phrase the facts. Language will scarce graze the skin — but here's a try.

The North American Indian, by and large, has never been notorious as a failure in war. Crude his methods may be, but they are effective. It has taken the "superior" white man's best efforts to subdue him, and it would never have been accomplished but for infinitely better weapons; for, later, superior numbers and a judicious use of whisky. Some tribes have naturally inclined to peace and endurance of wrong; some have fought fearfully at the pinch; and some are born butchers, hereditary slayers.

Foremost in the latter class has always stood the Apache. For warfare in his own domain he has been and is today without a peer. From time untold he has been pirate by profession, a robber to whom blood was sweeter than booty, and both as dear as life. Untold generations before the Caucasian outpost encroached upon his Sahara, he was driving his quartz-tipped shafts through the agricultural Aztec or peaceful Pueblo. The warlike tribes to his east and north too suffered from many a wild foray. From Guaymas to Pueblo and from San Antonio to where the Colorado laps the arid edge of California, he swept the country like a whirlwind. Of what he has done to keep his gory hand in since blonde scalps first amused his knife, I need not remind you now.

Not only is he the most war-loving of the American Indians, he is also the supreme warrior. The Bedouin of the New World, he is strong to an endurance impossible in a more endurable country. He has the eye of a hawk, the stealth of a coyote, the courage of a tiger — and its merci-lessness. His horse will subsist on a blade of grass to the acre, and will travel a hundred and ten miles in twenty-four hours without dropping dead at the finish. He knows every foot of his savage realm better than you know your own parlor. He finds food and drink where we should perish for want of both. Wherever you may strike him, he has a fastness, and one practically impregnable. Lay siege to him, and he quietly slips out some cañon back door and is away before you know it. The menace of the Indian moreover is in inverse ratio to his food supply. His whole life a ceaseless struggle to tear a living from nature, the Apache is whetted down to a ferocity of edge never reached by an Indian of a section where wood, water and game are ready to his hand. Why, a six-year-old Apache will ride a bronco farther in a day, and over rougher country, than you could ride the gentlest steed. These youngsters who were out with the hostiles were doing it right along.

This is not all that puts the Apache at the head of his class — he has comrades to stand in with him. From the outstretched hand of pursuit he slides down into Mexico as if the hills and valleys were a greased pole — taking time to murder, rob and ravish in transit. Once safely in Sonora, he sells his stolen stock without any trouble, caches the stolen arms, ammunition and money; enjoys a genteel holiday in the Mexican sierras until he is rested; swoops down upon hacienda and village, killing a few people and gathering up all the loot he can pack or drive; and flits back like a shadow to his Arizona strongholds. The better class of Mexican desires his extermination; even the lower classes sometimes organize against him; but he finds plenty of degraded natives to help him. The Mexican line is not only a boundary — it is a wholesale "fence." And sad to

8

say, some poor, mescal-corned *paisano* is not the Apache's only ally. In Tombstone, Tucson, and many another place on either side of the line, you will find white Americans who fatten on his bloody booty. If the list were published, certain Arizona merchants would writhe. At $20 a gallon, however, they willingly take their chances.

CHAPTER **II**

FORT BOWIE, headquarters of the cavalry, was founded in 1862 by the California Volunteers. It lies on a rather sharply sloping bench of the mountain-side, from which, down through a gap in the hills, one looks across the weird plain to the purple ranges fifty-three miles away. The post stands at an altitude of 4781 feet and is hemmed in by ranges on every side. Though there is neither fort nor fortification, it is called "Fort" Bowie. Behind it is the inevitable crag — in this case "Ellen's Dome" — from which a maiden threw herself to escape the Indians. You know the mountainous country which cannot boast some such legendary cliff is poor indeed. Around the generous plaza

10

stand big, substantial adobes, and at the farthest corner from the entrance, a French-roofed frame building of some pretensions, the residence of Colonel Beaumont, commander of the post. Good water is pumped by steam power from an adjacent hillside. There are about a hundred soldiers stationed here, and I fancy that they have a very fair sort of a time. The discipline is Number One, and everything is as trim and taut as a man o'war.

It was in these surroundings that I found Indian fighter Brigadier General George Crook. Since the Civil War no prominent commander has been more persistently, more savagely, more cruelly hounded by jealousy, opposition and many another masked influence than has George Crook. Almost without exception the Territorial papers have damned him — not with "faint praise," but with the bitterest invective. He has been cursed, belittled and lied about, his policy misrepresented, his acts distorted, and alleged acts of his have been made up out of whole cloth. Some of these lies — such as the one about his surrendering to the Apaches in the Sierra Madre in 1878 — have already been nailed. Others have not; some never will be. He is a soldier, not a war correspondent. Let the lying go as it will, telegraphed from end to end of the country — he never opens his mouth. He is here to fight, not to justify himself.

No man whose heart quickens to honor and courage but must admire the grim old General. There is that in him that makes one want to take off one's hat. There never was a soldier who fought with a stiffer lip against heavier odds. He has the same patient, persistent, uncomplaining and unapologetic doggedness that was Grant's fundamental characteristic. Today the most prominent figure in the army — the only army in the field — he occupies a larger place in public discussion than any other general. And in this exposed position, one of the fiercest fires is centered on him that ever whistled about a soldier's ears. It is the old story of political chicanery, greed and intrigue.

It is like pulling teeth to get anything out of him, however, and in his own defense he will not utter a word. He feels it, no doubt. He would be more than a man if the poisoned shafts did not sting. Yes, the old man carries other wounds than the Apache arrow that still rankles in his thigh — but you would never know it from him. Every time I look at him some half-forgotten lines come to my mind. They describe the old gray wolf at bay. Who wrote them, you who are nearer Bartlett's *Familiar Quotations* may hunt up:

> And when the pack, loud-baying,
> His bloody lair surrounds,
> He dies in silence — biting hard
> Amidst the yelping hounds.

Not that there is anything of the ferocity of the wolf about Crook. As kindly as he is reticent, he is not even bluff. But it is the same unwhimpering grit, the same deathless hold. In appearance the head of the Department of Arizona is a tall, well-knit man without one ounce of superfluous flesh. Though straight, he does not convey that impression, for his well-turned head has the peculiar droop of the habitual thinker. It is as though the weight of care and thought behind the seamed forehead carried it forward from its poise. The deep, clean lines that mark his face are further tokens of the hard brainwork he has put into his campaign. He is an indefatigable worker and keeps at the problems of the day well into the night. His heavy brown beard is again usurping his chin, which a few weeks ago was shaven. His forehead is high and broad; his eyes clear and penetrating; his nose large and very strongly aquiline. He wears nothing to denote his rank or even his profession, but paces thoughtfully up and down the porch in a plain neatly-kept civilian suit and a big buff slouch hat.

No, he is no bullion-lace, Sunday soldier, this Brigadier General George Crook. The furrows that seam his thoughtful face today show that his brain has not been vacationing these direful years. They have been earned. Running up against the physical impossibility of corraling the hostiles, he has done the next best thing — kept them always on the jump. They could still put a passing pellet through some lonely ranchero, but Crook has kept it too hot for them to get away plunder-laden. And there he has them on the hip. It was that policy that finally enabled him to bring in the last of the Chiricahua* renegades and establish them upon the reservation, where for two years their record was one of peace and prosperity. But Crook also had to contend with the interested misrepresentation and vilification, against the greed, the heartlessness, and the malice of men of his own race, and finally the famous outbreak of Geronimo and Natchez which need not have happened had matters been left in Crook's hands. No man has ever better known the Indian, no man has been more capable of handling him. "The Indian is a peculiar institution," Crook said. "And still, he is a human being. A good many persons seem anxious to forget that fact."

Yes, noble old Roman that George Crook is, his silent, unflinching heroism in the face of official setbacks, newspaper lies, and civilian malevolence, makes my blood tingle. If ever there was an honorable task in letting in the light on a libeled career, it lies before me now.

· · · ·

When I arrived here we all supposed the campaign at an end. On March 25 a truce had been made, and two days later all the hostiles, a hundred and five men, women and children, including Chihuahua, Mangas, Natchez, Geronimo and Nanay, had surrendered to Crook. But on the twenty-ninth Natchez and Geronimo and about thirty others slipped away during a rainstorm — after drinking whisky thoughtfully supplied by a fellow named Tribolet

---

* Lummis came to feel that Chihuicahui was the correct rendering of the name and used only this spelling in his later work. Here, however, his spelling has been made consistent and the more familiar Chiricahua has been used.

14

who lives in Sonora, just below the line. This fact stands unmoved, but I see somebody has been sending off dispatches to anti-Crook papers setting forth that Tribolet is a very nice man, one of the oldest residenters in the vicinity of Tombstone, wealthy, respected, etc. So I feel constrained to devote a bit more space to showing what man's lust for gold has done.

As long as the Apache wars last there are great and profitable contracts to be made. Consider that the continuance of the Apache wars means that more than $2,000,000 annually is disbursed within Arizona's borders by the War Department. Remove the army necessitating this expenditure, and wherewith would Arizona hide her nakedness? What industry has she to fall back on? What crutch of manufacture wherewith to hobble? Cattle she has on the oases of her vast deserts; but all Arizona can't be cowboy. As for the mining interests, not a mine in Arizona is today making money over and above expenses and current rates of interest on cost of plant.

The lonely ranchero honestly wishes this cruel war were over. So does the outlying farmer. So do the menaced miner and all who fear the confiscation of their own — or a related — scalp. The Arizonans who would be willing (with Artemus Ward) to sacrifice all their wife's relations to perpetuate their chief source of revenue are undoubtedly in the minority, but they make a majority noise. The longer the war can be kept up, bloodlessly, with just enough menace to excuse the retention of a strong military force, the better it will suit the commercial part of Arizona. The words of the wail are for "protection," but the air is for patronage. Last January, for instance, some ten companies were brought here from the coast on Governor Zulick's allegation that they were needed to keep the *citizens* from

15

butchering every Apache on the reservation. In plain truth, there are not enough white men in Arizona to storm the White Mountain fastnesses, and what there are would no more try it than they would poke their heads in a bear-trap. The decent people of Arizona, the many who are not ordinarily heard from, resented the imputation that they could harbor so barbarous an intention, and resented it so vigorously that Zulick denied his own appeal for troops. But the troops came, and here they are yet — and Arizona is milking just so many more teats.

Take one single example, the case of the trader Tri-bolet. "That man," said Crook to me, "is the cause of this whole trouble now. If it had not been for his whisky, Geronimo's renegades would never have decamped, the whole thing would now be settled, and we should be reaping the results of nearly a year's arduous labor. Oh no, there's no way of dealing with Tribolet. He has been tried before, but bought his way out. If we had shot him down like a coyote, as he deserved, it would have raised a terrible row. Why, that man has a beef contract for our army!"

In those words Crook lays bare a whole section of our national disgrace. The government is obliged to advertise and let the contracts to the lowest bidder. Tribolet got one. "It doesn't make any difference how big a scoundrel a man may be," Crook continued. "That doesn't disqualify him. Punish him by law? We have no laws here! This is a country where the majority rules, and no matter what is on the statute books, no law can be enforced against the sentiment of the community. And such fellows can undo the work of a great government, while we have no recourse." I hope that those of us who like to boast of our nation to the detriment of those across the seas will remember what customs officer Green told me. Tribolet told me himself that he didn't want the hostiles captured. 'Why,' said he, 'it's money in my pocket to have those fellows out.' And he bragged how much whisky he had sold them and how he had given Geronimo a bottle of champagne."

Yet Crook has always said, "In dealing with the Indian, you must first of all *be honest.*" Another rule Crook follows in dealing with the Indian is never to give him a grievance to brood over. "Settle the thing upon the spot," he said. "These little grievances are trifles in themselves, but they're like little worms boring into a big oak. The last one brings it down. And people at large, who never see anything but the final touch exclaim, 'Why, what fiends to break out for such a trifle!'"

In warfare with the Indians it has been Crook's policy — and the only effective one — to use them against each other. "To polish a diamond there is nothing like its own dust," he told me. "It is the same with these fellows. Nothing breaks them up like turning their own people against them. They don't fear the white soldiers, whom they easily surpass in the peculiar style of warfare which they force upon us, but put upon their trail an enemy of their own blood, an enemy as tireless, as foxy, and as stealthy and familiar with the country as they themselves, and it breaks them all up. It is not merely a question of catching them better with Indians, but of a broader and more enduring aim — their disintegration.

"The invention of the breech-loading gun and the metallic cartridge has entirely transformed the methods and the nature of Indian warfare. It is not many years ago that the Indians were miserably armed, but all that has changed. They are no longer our inferiors in equipment. Instead of bows and lances, they now have the best makes of breech-loading guns and revolvers. For white soldiers to whip the Chiricahuas in their own haunts would be impossible. The enormous country which they range is the roughest in America and probably in the world. It is almost utterly bare of anything upon which a white man could exist, but it supplies everything the Chiricahuas need to prolong life indefinitely. There is no end of the mescal plant everywhere in their territory, and if there were nothing else whatever, the Apache could live very comfortably on the varied products of that wonderful plant. He has no property which he cannot carry along in his swiftest marches, no home to leave at the mercy of his enemies. He roves about like the coyote, as unencumbered and more elusive. He knows every foot of his territory, and can live through fatigue, lack of food and of water which would kill the hardiest white mountaineer. By the generalship which they have found necessary, they oblige us always to be the pursuers, and unless we can surprise them, the odds are all in their favor.

"When it comes to a fight, for instance, we can't see anything of our foe — nothing but the puffs of their rifles. Nothing is exposed but here and there an eye, peering from behind some rock. *You* can't see that eye but those fellows, with their marvelous vision, will see your eye at a hundred yards. No white man can take advantage of the ground as they do. Our soldiers have to expose themselves, since they are the attacking party. As a sample of their fighting, look at the time when those Mexican banditti attacked Crawford. When they first fired into the camp in which our scouts were sleeping, they wounded two men in bed. The scouts took to the rocks, and in an hour and a half or two hours of hard firing by a hundred and fifty Mexicans, not one of those scouts got so much as a scratch. When the

Mexicans shot down Crawford, however, a few of the nearest scouts dropped eight out of the nine Mexicans who did it, at a volley. If they hadn't been checked by Maus, they'd have wiped that Mexican force off the face of the earth.

"No, to operate against the Apache we must use Apache methods and Apache soldiers — under, of course, the leadership of the white soldier. The first great difficulty is to discover the whereabouts of the hostiles, and this can be done well only by Indian scouts. Their stronghold once located, the next thing is to reach it secretly. The marches must be made with the utmost stealth and by night. Fires and noise are absolutely prohibited. The Indian scouts must be kept far enough in front and on the flanks to discover the enemy without being seen themselves, leaving no trail whatever, but slinking along from cover to cover. As soon as they locate the hostile camp, they noiselessly surround it if possible, meantime sending runners back to us. We make forced marches by night, come up and attack the hostiles, if they have not already flown. It is impossible to pursue them, for every rock may hide an Apache at bay, and with his breechloader he can kill as many pursuers as he pleases, himself secure. Then there is nothing for us to do but to return to our base of supplies, wait until the hostiles begin to feel secure again, and then repeat the same tedious operation. A single element of precaution neglected, and failure is certain.

"Without Apache scouts we could have made no progress. I first began using them in 1872, and have used them ever since. Nothing has ever been accomplished without their help. Have they acted in good faith? We have every assurance that they have. They followed the hostiles' trails almost as well as bloodhounds. It is nonsense to think that white trailers could have done the work. These white mountaineers howl against the Apache scouts — but how does it happen that they and the cowboys together never killed a hostile? The scouts have put in on the chase the most tremendous work men ever did; and when they succeeded in catching up with the hostiles, they have invariably fought well. But there is a great uproar because the Chiricahuas have been employed as scouts. There is a reason for their employment. A good many people think that any Indian scout will do, but this is not so. The average Indian scout is almost invariably better in his peculiar line than a white man, but the ordinary Indian, and even the ordinary Apache, is totally unable to cope with the Chiricahua. The White Mountain Apache comes nearest to it, being a mountain Indian also. But the Chiricahua is matchless. How much this may be due to his having been on the warpath more than the others and never having been thoroughly thrashed, I cannot say, for it is the warpath that brings out the qualities of the Indian and puts the keen edge on him. At all events, the Chiricahua is the supreme scout — and all the other tribes acknowledge it."

This opinion of Crook's is corroborated by everyone who has had to do with Apaches. It is a fact that for nearly a year the Apaches on the reservation have not dared to send their hunting parties out into the surrounding mountains for fear the renegades might slip up from Mexico and swoop down upon them. Crook had Tonto, Yuma, Mojave, San Carlos, White Mountain, Warm Springs and Chiricahua Apaches — all good — in his forces, but the Chiricahuas far surpassed the rest. Major Davis took a command of cavalry along on his first expedition, but on his second left the cavalry behind. He found it only an encumbrance. It was good cavalry, too — but it couldn't keep up with the scouts, and while it never so much as saw a hostile, the scouts overtook and killed several.

Captain Dorst, after his return from the campaign in Mexico, told me it was simple idiocy to try to do anything down there without Indian scouts. "No one else knows anything about that untravelled country," he said. "No one else can follow a trail as they can, and no one else can stand so much fatigue. My scouts will start at the bottom of a steep mountain, fifteen hundred feet high, and go on a trot clear to the top without stopping. There isn't a white man alive who could run fifty yards up the same pitch without stopping to catch his wind. I have been climbing the mountains of Colorado, New Mexico and Arizona for the last seven years, but I can't keep in sight of these fellows when they start."

I may add that the howl against Apache scouts comes largely from alleged white scouts of the Frank Leslie stamp, who want the positions for themselves. The real white scouts, men like Al Seeber or Frank Bennett, cheerfully admit that Apache scouts are indispensable.

CHAPTER III

I HAVE NOW the real particulars of the surrender and the escape, together with the speeches made by the Apaches on the occasion of the surrender and taken down verbatim on the spot.

Having received the news from Lieutenant Maus that Geronimo desired to give himself up [March 1886 — T. L. F.], General Crook immediately started for the San Bernardino rancho. This lies partly in Arizona but mostly in Mexico, near the point where the lines of New Mexico, Old Mexico, and Arizona come together. He was accompanied by Captain Bourke, Major Roberts and Master Charlie Roberts, a bright and nervy lad of eleven. They

traveled in an ambulance, with relays and no escort, reaching the line in ninety miles. Thence they went by saddle twenty-five miles in Sonora, arriving at Lieutenant Maus's camp on the morning of March 25. Geronimo and his band, camped in an impregnable stronghold upon a cañon-cleft hill a quarter of a mile from Maus, saw them arrive. He sent word that he wanted to come down and have a talk with Crook. Before a reply could be got to him, he came down, accompanied by Nachita (commonly called Natchez) and several bucks. Geronimo (his Indian name is Góy-ath-lay, "Man-Who-Yawns") said he wanted to talk with Gray Fox. "I am not here to talk with you," Crook replied, "but to hear you talk." Geronimo began a long-winded palaver, explaining why he had gone on the warpath.

Crook promptly shut him up, saying, "Geronimo, you are a liar. You have lied to me once, and I cannot believe you any more. You must decide at once to surrender unconditionally, or to stay in the mountains. If you decide to stay in the mountains, you may be sure that every last man of you will be hunted down and killed, if it takes us fifty years. Go back to your village and think it over, and let me know what you decide. I want no delay about it."

Geronimo was terribly taken aback at this reception of his overtures. He pulled nervously at a string, and big drops of sweat stood out on his hands and forehead. He returned with his companions to their fastness to chew the cud of deliberation. During this conference, Chihuahua, the brains of the band, got back with his bucks from a raid in Sonora, driving a few ponies, and joined Geronimo in the hills. The next morning Chihuahua sent word to General Crook that the bucks had been talking together all day, but had not yet reached a decision. It made no difference what the rest did however, he was going to surrender anyhow, and would come in that noon with his followers, if Crook would allow. But the Gray Fox was too shrewd to give his consent. There was the very leaven he wished to be working in the Apache camp; and he sent word to Chihuahua that none would be received until all surrendered.

The following day they all came in — that is all the chiefs, Geronimo, Kut-le, Chihuahua, Nanay and Nachita, with a few bucks — to meet Crook. It was an interesting scene, down amid the savage wilderness of the Cañon de los Embudos, the army men on the one hand, the superbly conditioned Chiricahuas on the other, and the peace of the whole Southwest hanging on their conference. Geronimo, his face blackened (as was that of Kut-le) by galena, sat under a mulberry. Besides Crook there were present Captain Bourke, Major Roberts and son, Lieutenants Maus and Faison, Dr. Davis, ex-Mayor Strauss of Tombstone, Mr. Moore, master of transportation; Mr. Daly, about eighty of Maus's Apache scouts and Mr. Fly, a nervy photographer from Tombstone. There were also interpreters. Chihuahua spoke first. The literal translation of his speech almost reminds one of a paragraph from Cooper. Chihuahua was talking for his life, and there is pathos as well as poetry in his flights.

"I am very glad to see you and have this talk with you," he said. "It is as you say—we shall always be in danger so long as we remain out here. But I hope from this time on we may live better with our families, and not do harm to anybody. I am anxious to behave. I think the sun is looking down upon me, and the earth is listening. I am thinking better. It seems to me that I have seen the one who makes the rain and sends the winds — or he must have sent you to this place. I surrender myself to you because I believe in you, and you have never lied to us. You do not deceive us. You must be our God. I am satisfied with what you do. You are, I think, the one who makes the green pastures, who sends the rain and commands the winds. You must be the one who sends the fresh fruits that come on the trees every year. There are many men in the world who are great chiefs and command many people; but you must be the greatest of all, or you would not come out here to see us. I want you to be a father to me and treat me as your son. I want you to have pity on me. There is no doubt that all you do is right, because all you do is just the same as if God did it. All you do is right. So I consider you to be. I trust in all you say. You do not lie. You do not deceive.

25

All the things you tell us are so. Now I am in your hands. I place myself at your disposal. I surrender myself to you — do with me as you please. I shake your hand [grasping Crook's hand]. I want to come right into your camp with my family and stay there. I don't want to be away at a distance. I want to be right where you are. I have run in these mountains from water to water. I have never found a place where I could see my father or my mother, till today when I see you, my father. I surrender to you now, and I don't want any more bad feeling or bad talk. I am going to stay with you in your camp.

"Whenever a man raises anything, even a dog, he thinks well of it and tries to raise it right, and treats it right, even if it *is* a dog. So I want you to feel towards me and be good to me. Don't let people say bad things about me. Now I surrender to you and go with you. When we are traveling together on the road or anywhere else, I hope you will talk to me sometimes. I think a great deal of Alchesay and Keowtennay [two of Crook's Apache scouts], and they think a great deal of me. I hope some day to be the same as their brother, and that you will think the same of me as you do of them. I would like you to send my family with me wherever you send me. I have a daughter at Camp Apache [the reservation] and other relatives of my companions and me. Wherever you want to send me, I wish you would send them. How long will it be before I can live with these friends?"

I have remarked that Chihuahua is the brains of the band. You will see from the above that he is also the orator. General Crook told him that his family should accompany him if they wished.

Then Nachita talked in words which are by interpretation as follows: "What Chihuahua says, I say. I give you my word, I give you my body, I surrender. I have no more to say than that. When I was free, I gave orders, but now I surrender to you. I throw myself at your feet. You order now, and I obey. What you tell me to do, I must do."

Geronimo followed: "Two or three words are enough. I have little to say. I surrender myself to you [shaking Crook's hand]. We are all companions, all one family, all one band. What the others say, I say also. Now I give myself up to you. Do with me what you please. I surrender. Once I moved about like the wind. Now I surrender to you, and want to be the same as if I was in your pocket. Now I feel like your brother, and Keowtennay is my brother also. I was very far from here. Almost nobody could get to that place. But I sent you word I wanted to come in here, and here I am. Whatever you tell us is true. We are all sure of that. I hope the day will come when my word is as strong with you as yours is with me."

Nanay and Kut-le then surrendered. Crook asked the chiefs if the surrender included all their people. They said it did. Then followed a general confabulation, in which the prisoners asked to be taken back to the fort by easy marches, as their stock was worn out. Crook promised. The bucks, squaws and children came in during the night, and before morning all ninety-two hostiles were prisoners.

Now for the unhappy sequel. There is no doubt that Geronimo and his band surrendered in good faith. They had no other reason for giving themselves up but that they were tired of the war and glad to come in and take their chances. Whatever disposition might be made of them, they knew that Crook would give them fair play. This absolute confidence of the Indians in his honor is almost as important a factor in Crook's success as his matchless knowledge of their traits. They would not have surrendered

27

thus to any other man. All was serene; but one of the same malign influences which from year to year have fanned the savage spark to the blaze of war again got in its work.

The great San Bernardino rancho runs from the Sulphur Springs valley, this side of the line, down many leagues into Sonora. The surrender took place on it, twenty-five miles below our boundary. On this rancho, some four hundred yards below the line, lives a Swiss-American, named Tribolet — long notorious in Tombstone as a fence for rustlers. He was tried, some years ago, for stealing barley from the government at Fort Hauchuca. It isn't easy even yet to convict a man in this Territory, and he got off. He is still deemed a fence; and, what is infinitely worse, furnishes whisky to the Indians. He makes no secret of it and snaps his fingers at protests. On the day before the surrender, it was noticed that Geronimo and other bucks were getting pretty full. It has since been discovered that Tribolet had smuggled five five-gallon demijohns to a secret place near their fastness. They surrendered all right, however, and came along handsomely with Crook as far as Smugglers' Springs, where they camped on the night of the twenty-ninth. There, despite all possible precautions to keep them from it, they came in contact with more of Tribolet's whisky. Some of Maus's Indian scouts had smashed this white scoundrel's whisky barrels, and destroyed all the liquor in sight, yet nevertheless more whisky had been brought out and gotten to the hostiles. Tribolet and his emissaries played also upon the fears of the prisoners, telling them they were putting their necks into the halter by going along with the soldiers. Savage as the Apache is, there are matters in which he is a perfect child. Take him in the night, especially when he is tipsy, and the veriest vagabond's ghost story will stampede him. Of course, you

28

will understand from what has already been said of the Apache that Lieutenant Maus's eighty-four men were entirely inadequate to surround, bind or disarm the ninety-two prisoners. It would have taken a thousand men to make even a stagger at doing it, and even then many a life would have been lost in the operation. At the faintest hint of either move, the Apaches would have been off like a flock of quail.

The whisky conspirators succeeded. That night, during a rainstorm, Geronimo and Nachita, accompanied by twenty other bucks and fourteen squaws — one an immature girl — slipped out of camp noiselessly, and, breaking their trail on rocks, fled into the most impassable mountains.

CHAPTER **IV**

THE CHIRICAHUA APACHES who surrendered to General
Crook on March 29 and arrived here April 3 will be sent
to Fort Marion, St. Augustine, Florida, as prisoners of war.
The squaws and children go too, making seventy-six in
all.

I have never told you about the pow-wow on the day
when the prisoners came in. We were all watching, that
day, for their arrival. At last, just before noon, over a high
ridge on the Bear Springs trail from the south, a grotesque
figure came out against the sky. Down the rough slope
toward us it came, soon another popped up over the horizon, and so on for half an hour. Lieutenant Faison and Dr.

30

Davis rode at the head of the straggling procession, and the rest came as it chanced, bronco bucks (as the male hostiles are called), scouts, women and children, sometimes within a rod of each other, and sometimes with a hundred yards of interval. Stopping only for a brief greeting, they rode up to headquarters and then on down to the arroyo to make camp. Later in the afternoon, Chihuahua came up with Alchesay and Keowtennay (he spells it Ka-e-te-na, but I have adopted the phonetic spelling, as Apache has no rules) for a talk with Crook. Alchesay and Keowtennay are two friendly Apache chiefs — and valuable, indeed, have been their services in this campaign. The conference was held in

31

General Crook's private office. Present, the General in a rawhide-seated chair; Major Roberts, his adjutant; Keowtennay, in another cow-chair; Alchesay, on the floor next to my camp-stool; Chihuahua, squatted against a side door, with his knees up and touching and his feet apart; José María, an old Mexican, who *sabes* only his own language and Apache; and Mr. Montoya, a Mexican who speaks good English. It was a roundabout conversation. General Crook would ask a question in English; Montoya would put it into Spanish; María snatch it up and twist it into Apache; Alchesay or Keowtennay would answer, and then it went through the reverse process till it came out in plain United States.

Questioned about Geronimo's stampede after the surrender, Keowtennay said that the first unpleasantness came the night before the surrender, when they had gotten hold of Tribolet's whisky and were filling up. Someone flirted with one of Nachita's squaws. Jealous, Nachita shot the woman through the knee with a six-shooter. On the night of the stampede Chihuahua, Keowtennay, and Alchesay camped close to Lieutenant Maus. Geronimo, Nachita and their immediate followers settled upon a hill a short distance off. None knew of the escape until next morning. The fugitives took so few women because more would burden their flight. Nachita would undoubtedly get lonely, as he is fond of a good many fat young squaws, like the good-looking one he took along.

Chihuahua said he thought it very likely that Nachita will return, though it is a *quien sabe* case. He didn't believe, however, that Geronimo will ever be seen again.

After General Crook had asked all the questions he wished and was about to dismiss the meeting, Chihuahua, who has a very kindly face and musical voice, hitched forward several feet toward the General, and said he wanted to talk a little.

"When a man thinks well, he shows it by his talk. I have thought well since I saw you. Ever since you were so kind to me in the mountains [at the surrender] my heart has quieted down. My heart is very quiet now. Geronimo has deceived me as much as he did you. I was very glad when I saw my sons and wife. I think well of my family, and want to stay with them. Those who ran off did not think well of their families, nor show love. I am a man that whenever I say a thing I comply with it. I have surrendered to you. I am not afraid of anything. I have to die sometime. If you punish me very hard, it is all right. I am much obliged to you for your kindness. I have surrendered to you and thrown away my arms. I didn't care any more for my gun or any other weapon. [This is true. The old fellow didn't have so much as a knife, all the time he was here.] I surrender to you, and ask you to have pity on me. You and nearly all your officers have families, and think very much of them, as I do mine, and I want you to remember your families. I hope you will not punish me very hard, but pity me. I have been very happy since I saw my family again [they have been prisoners here for some months]. I was sleeping very quiet and happy with my family at Camp Apache [at the reservation] but Geronimo came and deceived me, played me a trick and made me leave. Wherever you put me, keep me away from Geronimo and his band. I want nothing to do with them. People will talk bad about me and get me into trouble. I don't want anything to do with him. I was very quiet and happy at Camp Apache, looking after the little crop which I had in the ground, and my horses and wagons, but Geronimo came along and told me so many lies that I had to go [this is strictly true].

33

It is true that we have stolen many cattle and horses, and done many depredations, but Geronimo is to blame for all we did. Now I have surrendered to you I am quiet and happy. It is very good to see my children, and I want to live happy and quiet all the time. That is all."

There have been many other little pow-wows between Crook and the Indians here, but none of particular interest until last Tuesday, the day before the prisoners were sent off. That afternoon Noche, Dutchy (who killed the slayer of Captain Crawford last January), Stove Pipe, Charley and other scouts were squatted upon the porch at headquarters. The interpreters sat upon chairs, the General on another, tilted back against a window. He was tired and preoccupied. The Indians had been chattering at him for a couple of hours with their childish requests. Most of them wanted letters written to their friends on the reservation, telling when they'd get home. Others had directions to send about the care of a horse or a hoe. Crook listened patiently and arranged their little perplexities. Then he gave them a little valedictory, for several weeks ago he had written to Washington, asking to be relieved, and a few days after I got here, the telegram granting his request had arrived.

"I am going to leave you," he said. "Another officer is coming in my place [sensation in the audience]. I want to thank you for the good work you have done. You have been very faithful. I have made many enemies among my own people by being honest and square with you. After I am gone, probably some will tell you lies about me. But you must judge me by my acts. Talk is cheap. I hope you will remember the good advice and teachings I have given you. Do everything to stop this tizwin-drinking. You get it in your stomachs, and there is no sense left. Then you go and gamble away all your money, and the next day there is nothing to show for it but a swelled head [laughter]. Go to raising stock, as well as the farming you have already learned. You will do better to raise sheep than cattle. To get anything out of a steer you have to kill him; but you can sell the wool off your sheep, and still have the sheep [approbative chorus of "Hu! Hu!"]. Then the sheep, though they have to be watched, will not wander off great distances as the cattle will ["Hu! Hu!"]. Besides, you know if thieves come and run off a few of your cattle, it is hard to get them again; but when a few sheep go, they travel very slowly, so you can easily catch them and the thief [very emphatic "Hu! Hu!"].

Chihuahua, whose bright little boy had been nudging and crawling over him, spoke now as follows:

"I am glad that you will talk to us. As soon as I saw you down there in the mountains, it seemed to me that I had quieted down very suddenly. My heart got very quiet. After I saw you, I slept well that night, and drank nothing but water. It seemed to me as if I had suddenly got well from some disease. Since I surrendered to you I have been very quiet and contented. You can do a great deal of good to me. I am very glad because all you tell me is right. I am very much satisfied to be with my family. I believe every word you tell me. Wherever you send me it is all right. My children cry a great deal to think of leaving two horses I have, and I would like to take them with us. I would like to know when you are going to send us away, so I can collect some money the scouts owe me."

General Crook: "Well, you'd better collect it right away."

Chihuahua: "We would like to have an officer go with us."

General Crook: "I will send a good one with you, and one who can talk Spanish."

Chihuahua: "I am satisfied and content, wherever you send me. I think all my people will behave all right, and I hope sometime to come back and see my people. They gave me a good wagon at the reservation, and I am afraid that if I am gone a very long time, I cannot get the wagon again when I come back."

General Crook: "Oh, I'll tell your relatives to take care of that."

Poor old Chihuahua thanked him and trotted off, evidently feeling blue. His talk indicates the naive childishness of his race in some points, rugged and self-reliant as they are in others. The guarantee of his utter honesty lies in his acts. He could have escaped with all his people a hundred times from the camp here. They could have escaped en route to the train later. But they didn't make the slightest offer of it, though they had a good many forebodings as to what would be done with them. So far as their own honor is concerned, they could be safely sent to Florida without a single guard. But soldiers will be necessary to protect these poor savages from the "civilized" whites along the way. Why, General Crook wouldn't let me telegraph that they were going, until the night before they went, for this very reason. There are plenty of alleged white men who would signalize their bravery by shooting a captive squaw through a car window, if they had received sufficient notice to brace themselves with brag and whisky. Here, too, you can see the advantage of honest dealing with an Indian. These people trust Crook, and faithfully, in turn, keep their pledges to him. It was fortunate, for all the troops at Fort Bowie and Bowie Station wouldn't have been enough to disarm and bind those

Apache prisoners. In fact the history of the "captives" has been that of a people on parole, rather than of prisoners. The Territorial papers howled and damned Crook for a fool, but the logic of events sets him clear and clean above their malice. Instead of trying what he knew was impossible, killing a few women and children, losing all the warriors to be again hunted, he gave his word and got theirs, and they did not fail him. He did have trusty men camped with the prisoners to talk down any dissatisfaction, but that is all.

The remark made by the scouts when Crook told them of the official change is significant. They said, "We don't know this man that is coming instead of you. What is he? Is he a good man, or will he lie to us the same way other white people have lied to us? We would like you to write us a letter telling him that we have done right, and to do right with us."

General Crook assured them that his successor would be a good and honest man, and promised to recommend them to him. It is a pitiful commentary on our civilization that the Apaches have been so lied to and swindled that they don't know whom to trust, and are suspicious of any man until they have tested him and found him of honest metal, as they have Crook.

CHAPTER V

WHEN THEY WERE brought to the fort, the broncos (as hostile Chiricahuas are termed in contradistinction to the scouts) camped behind a hill about three-quarters of a mile from the fort. They chose the bed of a dry arroyo, and settled down contentedly among the tufts of bear-grass and cactus. Firewood and rations were hauled down to them, and they utilized both to the utmost. The women and children captured by Captain Crawford and Captain Davis some months ago, and since held prisoners at this post, were let out and rejoined their relatives and friends with demonstrative welcomes. All but one, that is. There was one good-looking girl who wept bitterly at the pros-

pect of being released from the guard-house and appealed
to General Crook to let her stay. It seems that her husband
was killed in one of the raids last year; and she fore-
saw that if she rejoined the band, in which she had no
relatives, she would be kicked from pillar to post, and
have to work like a slave to be tolerated at all. The General
granted her request. The captives did not do much the first
day except to build their fires and inter their rations. Next
day, however, they began to change the aspect of things.
The patient squaws knotted back the rambling bear-grass
with strings of its own tough fibre, grubbed out the immediate cactus, dragged in branches of scrub oak and

39

mesquite, and made semicircular wind-breaks four or five yards from point to point. Against these were laid the blankets, the soiled canvas and other "furniture."

Here and there you would see a squaw bracing up some stalks of the century plant and lashing them together at the top, while her sister in drudgery was stitching together big lengths of unbleached muslin. After two days of this hard work — to which the bucks lent their moral support by industriously gambling at coon-can for cartridges, money or ponies, or by promenading along the fort — the camp was complete. One palace which flapped in the breeze was constructed from horse blankets stretched from the top of a little scrub-oak; another was composed of a few rods of muslin tented over a peak of aloe stocks; and still another was a recess in the steep bank, with some sheeting stretched across the front from bush to bush, the skyward selvage soaring aloft on the point of a pole, the lower anchored down with rocks, with a row of mescal-cactus for the rear wall. It was an interesting village. Against every bush leaned a gun, maybe half a dozen. Every male Indian over three feet high wore one, two or three cartridge belts, filled with the overgrown 45-70 cartridges of Uncle Sam's rifles; a butcher knife of Sheffield make, in a sheath which swallowed nearly all the handle as well as all the blade; a curious leather sheath in which is transported the indispensable awl for mending the moccasins; numerous bracelets and necklaces of big gay beads, and generally a small looking-glass and materials for improving the complexion according to Apache ideas. The bronco bucks were very shabbily dressed, as should be expected after the enormous hardships they have endured and the incredible distances they have made in the past ten months. Their average dress was a dirty print shirt, whose appendices toyed idly with the breeze, and they do a good deal of toying, for the breeze here for the last week has been one to sweep all the sand in Arizona over into New Mexico. Somewhere under the tailness of the shirt begins a pair of stout linen drawers, designed for white, but of a present color which is a monument to the vanity of earthly hopes. These draw closely around the ankles, so as to go inside the extremely tight-fitting moccasins. As the Apache travels in a cactus country, he cuts his moccasin accordingly. The toe, instead of coming to a flat point like a piece of pie, is strongly pug-nosed. Not only is the point turned up, but it has a little circular shield at the end, perpendicular to the ground and reaching two inches above it. This disc, as big around as a quarter, serves as a protection against thorns. The moccasin is not of shoe caliber like those of the Navajos, Pueblos, and other northern tribes, but has a leg about thirty inches long, the top of which is turned over so that it reaches to within three or four inches of the knee-pan. The assassinating cactus, which goes through ordinary shoe leather as 'twere a pleasure jaunt, is stumped by this elastic buckskin.

For the modest buck linen unmentionables do not suffice. Every one of them has a generous G-string whose extremities form small aprons front and rear. In fact this is a *sine qua non*. Those who chafe at the restraint of the underpants don't have to wear 'em. A good many robust broncos — and scouts, too, for that matter — have been parading about the post and camp in bare-kneed pantlessness, but without the G-string no one can hope to be admitted to polite Apache society. The headdress most in vogue is a big bandanna rolled to a band of two inches, and tied around the head to keep the long, black hair from the eye. In the evening or when riding in the cold a blanket or patchwork quilt is added to this costume. Chihuahua and a few of the others have once-gaudy Mexican serapes. The women wear calico dresses of uncertain denomination, but all modest. The Mother Hubbard seems to prevail only among the older women. The girls don't wear it. Their moccasin is similar to that of the men. The female children are women on a small scale, so far as dress goes; but the boys from little to big run around in the airy costume of shirt and G-string. Little fellows of seven or eight carry their cartridge belts and big knives; and one eleven-year-old had, when captured, a gun and a six-shooter. Master Apache, you see, gets his apprenticeship at piracy very early.

They are great hands for ornament but are not inclined to be captious about it. All of the scouts and most of the broncos had some silver trimmings; but when the silver ran short, other metals would do. The silver goes in Navajo style on their hats, belts and necklets. All the metal bracelets were brass, rather cleverly worked, and so were most of their rings. They go on the principle that a feast is as good as enough.

One "coffee-cooler" (as they call inferior, lazy scouts) whom I watched gambling had thirteen rings on his left hand, eleven on his right, and a dozen bracelets of beads and brass on each wrist. A good many of the girls supplemented their brass bracelets with tin ones made from old cans.

The Apaches are good-looking Indians. Chihuahua has as pleasant a face as one would care to meet, strikingly good natured and very intelligent. One or two have bad faces, but you can pick out worse on the streets of Los Angeles any day. There were five or six rather comely girls in the outfit. Old Nanay, a chunky, fat, superannuated chief, might readily be taken, so far as face goes, for a wealthy Mexican ranchero; and he is facile in a somewhat corrupted Spanish.

Among the most interesting of the captives is a fat, well-preserved, ever-smiling old squaw, wife of the celebrated Chief Mangas, and the mother, I believe, of nine children. She is generally called Francesca here (she was one of the guard-house party) but her real name is Sa-go-zhu-ni, which signifies "Pretty Mouth." She is an important personage in more ways than one. They say it is she who made the tizwin which led to the present outbreak. But now her ways are of peace — and population. She is the Juno of the tribe, and superintends the additions to the Chiricahua census. When Captain Bourke and I were down at the guard-house one day, before the arrival of the captives, she showed us a magical flint arrowhead, made from a peculiar stone found at a particular spot at a special season and possessed of great virtues in soothing ante-maternal pains. Last December one of the imprisoned squaws had a bouncing Christmas present, and some of the guards ran for the post surgeon. But old Francesca didn't require any foreign appliances or aid. When the doctor arrived the need for him was over. The necessary umbilical surgery had been performed with the sharp edge of a tomato can! Everyone supposed the poor little newcomer would directly turn up his toes to the daisies; but true Apache that he is, he is today as bright and vigorous a sprawler as you are apt to find anywhere.

Besides toying with the seductive coon-can, the Apache buck has a national game of his own. It is not so exciting as our baseball, nor so shinfully disastrous as Albion's cricket — but it is engrossing enough for him. It is the game of Na-joose. To a man up a mesquite bush, this recreation looks as rational as shaving the soles of your feet, but the Apache is content to stay with it all day. Upon a smooth bit of ground he builds two tiny straw piles thirty-five or forty feet apart and each with a little U-shaped depression on each side. The other machinery of the game consists of two poles, fifteen feet long, and looking for all the world like cane fish poles (each is made, however, of three straight willow sticks, most artistically spliced); and a six- or seven-inch hoop with a stout cord across its diameter. The two players stand elbow to elbow, about twenty or twenty-five feet from the straw pile toward which they are facing; and drop their poles until the taper tips bend upon the ground, the butts being held six or eight inches higher. One takes the hoop, holds it down between the poles, and with a deft toss sends it rolling. As it nears the straw pile, both players pitch their poles forward; and if it chances that the hoop falls across the poles near the butts, you will hear an approbative shout. Upon a closer look, the poles prove to have a series of notches cut along near the butt; while the hoop is similarly notched, and its cross string has little thongs drawn through the strands at certain intervals. The point of the game lies in which point falls upon which; and there is really room for much skill as well as a sufficiency of luck.

There also came under my observation a girl's game. They build a four-foot circle of fist-size stones, with three entrances. In the center of the circle is a flattish stone six or eight inches across. The three or four players squat around the outside of the circle, and each in her turn grasps three sticks, so shaped as to fit together in a round piece about eight inches long. She whacks these down smartly upon the central stone, tallying according to the distance and direction in which the sticks fly, and marking her score by moving a twig so many stones ahead in the circle.

The Apache buck has a more personal pastime as well. A fair portion of his day is devoted to personal decoration. Back in the recesses of a spavined tent or behind some wind-warding bush you stumble upon some bronze athlete artistically painting his face in vermillion streaks, rings, and blotches often crossed by a band of a micaceous pigment which glistens on the dark skin like a strip of steel. Or perchance he will be mollifying his great crop of hair with an egg-sized piece of mutton tallow — base barbarism which has not yet achieved the civilized refinement of rouge and perfumed lard!

Wildest in the rough sports of the bronco boys was one figure which you would single out at a glance. His sandy hair cropping out under a dirty cotton rag; his light skin, pretty liberally exposed, and everywhere a mass of miscegenated dirt and freckles, showed he was no Chiricahua. He was their little white captive, Santiago McKinn. The poor child, scaly with dirt, wild as a coyote, made my eyes a bit damp. His is a pathetic case. One day last summer, Geronimo and his band swooped down upon a little ranch on the Miembres [Mimbres — T. L. F.] River, above Deming, New Mexico. They did not attack the house, but skimmed along the range, where the two McKinn boys were herding cattle. The elder was killed, as nearly as we can learn, and Santiago, now eleven years old, was carried off. He has been with the Apaches ever since. But that is not what seems so pitiful. He has had to share their long marches, their scanty and uninviting fare, and all the hardships of such a life, no doubt; but he has not been maltreated. The Apaches are kind to their children, and have been kind to him. The sorrow is that he has become so absolutely Indianized.

It was almost impossible to get hold of him in camp. The Indian boys liked to be talked with; but let a white man approach, and Santiago would be off instanter. He understands English and Spanish (his father is Irish, his mother a Mexican), but it was hard labor to get him to speak either. Yesterday General Crook had an Apache bring him to Major and Mrs. Roberts' house. When told that he was to be taken back to his father and mother, Santiago began boo-hooing with great vigor. He said in Apache — for the little rascal has already become rather fluent in that language — that he didn't want to go back. He wanted to stay with the Indians. All sorts of rosy pictures of the delights of home were drawn, but he would have none of them, and acted like a wild young animal in a trap. When they lifted him into the wagon which was to take him to the station, he renewed his wails, and was still at them as he disappeared from view.

On the last evening before being sent to their Florida prison, General Crook's seventy-seven Chiricahua prisoners held a grand farewell dance under the floor-management of Chihuahua himself. The ballroom was a smooth spot on the eastern bank of the arroyo in which they were camped. It was brilliantly lighted by a huge bonfire of cord wood. The festivities began at nine o'clock, and were attended by broncos and scouts, not to mention a generous audience from the post. It was a wierd place for an evening's entertainment, there by the wild arroyo, up whose rocky sides the bristling cactus mingled with the tough mesquite, the wild, fantastic firelight dancing over the dusty soil, falling on gay blankets, glinting on a hundred handy gun-barrels, sparkling on a hundred buckled cartridge belts and shining on a hundred dark savage faces in shocks of midnight hair, and on nervous, taper hands (for all Chiricahuas have shapely hands) which had wrought death on many more victims than I like to remember.

The Chiricahuas were all in their best toggery and wrapped from the evening chill by bright-hued serapes, army blankets and even patch-work quilts. Every participant had also donned a brand new complexion. The medicine man was orchestra and conductor all in one. Hugging a crude little drum in the crook of his left elbow, he was surrounded by a dense circle of bucks four or five deep, who danced in a decorous shuffle to his taps, and sang in perfect unison with him. As nearly as I could catch their song, it went in this wise:

"Hai la-i,lai, ennay,
Nay, ennay,
Nay, ennay;
Hay nai, nay, nay ennay
Hai nay, nay, ennay,"

and so on for two hundred and thirteen verses or thereabouts. The bucks did not make any progress in their stepping, which was of a perpendicular, treadmill sort.

The belles of the ball, from simple six to sweet sixteen — for all the girls above infancy participated — were stationed a few yards higher up the slope than the men, while the non-combatant old women sat still further back in the shadows' verge. Every minute or two a pair of damsels would patter giggling down to the circle of dancers, slap two swains resoundingly on the shoulders, and scurry bashfully back. The two beaux thus favored would leave the circle, and each unfolding his blanket from his shoulders, share it with the girl who had elected him. Then all four would form a line — a buck at the extreme right facing from the circle, his partner facing toward it, next the other buck, facing from, and last of all, *his* girl, facing toward. Thus arranged, they would "sashay" up and down, now advancing clear up to the circle, and now retreating from it twenty-five feet or so. This would be kept up until the chorister stopped to catch his breath, when the bucks would return to the circle and the girls run laughing back to their companions. I don't know that it does the Apache beau any good to escape the ice-cream tribute which our belles demand, since he is in duty bound to give his dulcinea five or ten dollars for every night that she dances.

Far into the night the leaping ruddy fire threw its fantastic shadows about, while those savage merry-makers flitted here and there with jocund but depressing ululation.

The last morning in Arizona. All this morning the bronco camp was a scene of great confusion. The bucks were greasing their hair and gathering up their cartridges. The squaws were racing over the hills, catching and saddling the mules and horses and cleverly packing on them the blankets, muslin "tents," the pots and cups, canteens, baskets and hunks of jerked meat. Chihuahua, with his bright seven-year-old clinging on behind, was riding up and down all the time to hasten idlers. At 11:30, the camp was at last packed and afoot. A queer procession it was that wound down Apache Pass and out upon the dusty plain. Here was a gayly painted scout wearing the army blouse, a rifle or carbine across his saddle. Beside him perhaps was an equally painted bronco, equally well armed, but without the blouse. Next you might have seen a burro so hidden by big bundles that only his slender legs and comical head were visible, while on top and bestriding the whole aggregation would be a squaw, with the peculiar

Apache cradle under one arm and across her lap, the other hand being occupied with whip and bridle. One little pony carried a big buck, a solid squaw and a cradled baby.

General Crook accompanied them to Bowie station in a buckboard. All went cheerfully, although by now understanding what is to be done with them. The station was reached, the strange passengers were loaded into the emigrant sleepers, and now, stared at by tens of thousands of eyes, are trundling eastward toward their Florida prison.

CHAPTER **VI**

WELL, THE TENSION is over for the time being. What new excitement we are going to have can only be told by the last of the week. It is then that General Miles, Crook's successor, will arrive. It is believed by some that the new commander will pick up the whole force at his disposal and fling it at Mexican space at once, in hope of hitting Geronimo with scattering fragments. The more conservative opine that Miles will merely lay for the few remaining renegades, and whenever he sees a head, hit it. It would not surprise me at all if Geronimo and the rest of his band were to be brought in by General Miles shortly — but who paved the way? Who knocked the strength out of the rene-

gades? Who has sent to a Florida prison the most audacious and bloody raiders of them all, and three-fourths of their whole band? Who has chopped off the Apache hydra's chief heads — Ulzanna, Chihuahua and Kut-le; leaving only Geronimo, one good head, and Natchez, a dough-head? Why, old Nanay, fat, aged and lazy as he now is, was more force to the renegades than Natchez. If properly managed, the whole matter can be wound up very soon. But if a stranger comes in and fails to handle these unique savages with all the skill of a man who has dealt with and known them personally for fifteen years, will he be in the least to blame? General Miles, who has a superb reputation as an

Indian fighter, comes here under the vast disadvantage of unfamiliarity with the Apaches, their unparalleled wilderness, and their unparalleled methods of warfare. He will do his level best, there is no doubt of that; and I hope, however his efforts may result, that he will be given the fair play and honest treatment which have been denied General Crook.

You see, the closing work of General Crook's administration has put an entirely new face on the Apache situation. Instead of a hundred and ten dusky raiders, as there were two weeks ago, there are now but thirty-four and these somewhat weary of the fugitive existence they are forced to live. Instead of an army with six war chiefs there is now a handful of men with two leaders — Geronimo the foxy talker, and Nachita the hereditary chief, who is but a half-hearted warrior. Having been pursued ceaselessly for the past ten months, it is probable that they will now lurk in the far vastnesses of the Mexican mountains and not trouble our side of the line again. This is more likely from the fact that all their relatives have been put beyond their reach by the stroke of sending them to Florida. Had the captives been sent back to the reservation the outstanding hostiles would probably have raided it and got them out again, but now they have no show of getting reinforcements, nor even of recovering their families. This is apt to break the recalcitrants up. In fact I am inclined to believe that if the renegades could be communicated with today and told the exact facts, they would start for Fort Bowie tomorrow — all but perhaps Geronimo and three or four of his intimate followers — to give themselves up. Unluckily, one might as well try to telephone a comet.

General Crook is leaving here at his own request, and it is worse than foolish to construe his application for relief into an admission of failure, as some Territorial alleged newspapers have done. Crook can no more accomplish impossibilities than can any other mortal; but all that man can do, he has done.

When I told him that I was very sorry to learn that he was to leave, he said promptly and earnestly, "Well, *I'm* not. I have had to worry along with these fellows for eight years, and have got enough of them. Now let some others try their hands." That he is relieved not only officially but mentally and physically as well, I know. The long tension, the ceaseless vigilance, the continual grasping after the ungraspable, all have told on him. They would tell on iron. The Indians plague him to death, too. Scouts or captives, they hang around his quarters eternally. Their most trivial complaints, wishes or hopes, they insist on confiding to him, and with his gigantic patience, he listens to it all as kindly as a father could to the endless prattling of a child. It is tiresome enough, you may be sure, and the General has earned a rest in the department of his choice. (As ranking brigadier of the army he *had* his choice, and selected Omaha).

As a result of the farcical "news" that has been furnished the nation throughout, we have heard nothing but Geronimo, Geronimo, Geronimo. One would fancy that old Jerry was the only Apache who has been off the reservation; and there is not much question but that it would have made a bigger impression on the public if, instead of the seventy-six prisoners now rolling toward Fort Marion, Geronimo alone had been captured and all the rest were still at large. The fact is, Geronimo is only one of seven chiefs who have been off the reservation with their families and followers. He is not even a Number One chief, but merely a war chief, Nachita being the hereditary leader of the Chiricahaus. Nachita is an indecisive fellow, fonder of flirting than of fighting, greatly addicted to squaws, and rather easily led by Geronimo, who is a talker. Geronimo has not been the biggest fighter, the cleverest schemer, nor the bloodiest raider in the outfit at any time, until now, when only the dude Nachita is out with him. Chihuahua is smarter; Nanay, Kut-le and Ulzanna more bloodthirsty and more daring. Their bands have done more raiding and more mischief than Geronimo's. The only claim Geronimo has to his unearned pre-eminence of newspaper notoriety is that he is one of the originators of the outbreak. He is no greater and no worse than several of his co-renegades. History is so fashioned, however, that he will be remembered when his more important colleagues are forgotten.

•   •   •   •

Yesterday afternoon the boom of the six-pounder notified us that the ambulance containing the new commander of the Department of Arizona had rounded the bend in the road. In a few minutes more the six mules swung around the corner of the store and trotted up smartly across the sloping parade [ground?]. General Miles crawled out of the inadequate door of the ambulance in front of Colonel Beaumont's house and shook the kinks out of his legs. General Crook walked up from the office, and the two veterans shook hands undemonstratively.

Miles passed most of the afternoon in a close conference with General Crook, and this morning there was another pow-wow, General Miles gathering up all points as to the situation with which he is now to wrestle. While he and General Crook were talking, the Apache scouts came over to take their leave. The most prominent and valued ones — Noche, Charley, Dutchy, Stove-Pipe and others — trotted into the office with old Concepción and Lieutenant Maus.

They did a good deal of talking, and also had a short speech from General Miles. He reminded them how much better off they are than the renegades now lying among the mountains of Mexico and than the prisoners now in Florida. Every last one of the renegades, he informed them, will be hunted down and taken alive or dead, no matter how long it takes or how much money it costs; so he bade the scouts behave themselves when they got home.

It was a sight to see the scouts when they came to say farewell to Crook. The common "coffee-coolers" merely shook his hand very effusively, and said good-bye several times over. But the men whom he had trusted and who had proved their wonderful efficiency in this campaign were not content with that — they had to hug him.

Noche and Charlie, particularly, threw their arms around him and kept them there some time, patting him affectionately on the back with the right hand. He smiled at them indulgently and told them to be good Indians.

This noon they left us, steering their mules, horses and burros toward Camp Apache, where they will be disbanded as their enlistment has expired. The store of De Long, who got back last night from a long search through Mexico after bright-hued serapes for the scouts, was a busy place this morning, and by midday the majority of the scouts were clad in colors that would have knocked Solomon silly. All of them had plenty of cash, having just received four months' pay, and they made it fly. One, who had annexed to his store the proceeds of a little judicious coon-can, went out this morning and bought three extra horses for a hundred and sixty-six dollars. He had two hundred and fifty dollars more to go on, too.

There was a funny little incident just before they started off. A white fellow had sold a horse to one of the scouts.

55

Shorty found the animal a scrub and yearning to get his fingers again on his forty dollars, sought out the seller in the store and demanded his coin. White man requested him to go to Sheol. Scout said, "Come out, look horse. Dam' no good." White man came out, said he "didn't see no flies on that 'ere hoss," and started back to the store. But Shorty collared him, and beckoning at his pocket, said, "Come, money; come, money." White man tried to get away, but Shorty held on. At last the fellow caved, and paid over the forty dollars with an ill grace, remarking, "I'll meet you somewhere else one o' these times, an' then I'll fix you." The surrounding scouts roared in derision, well knowing what sort of a show the white man would stand against one of them. Shorty smiled sarcastically. "All right," he said. "When you want fight me? You catch him, you have him." Which was as pithy a retort as could be thought up to fit this matter of fighting the Apaches — "You *catch* him, and you can have him."

At one o'clock the ambulance and its sextette of long-ears was drawn up in front of Major Roberts' house. Several unassuming bundles in canvas were strapped behind, and then an old linen duster appeared at the door — and General Crook was bidding farewell to the group on the piazza. If ever cordial good wishes from those who were in a position to know him followed a man from the scene of his labors, they followed this one. When the doings of this decade have been refined from prejudice into history, when the mongrel pack which has barked at the heels of this patient commander has rotted a hundred years forgotten — then, if not before, Crook will get his due. In all the line of Indian fighters from Daniel Boone to date, one figure will easily rank all others — a wise, large-hearted, large-minded, strong-handed, broad-guage man — George Crook.

I am glad that, after a third of a century of almost steady campaigning, he has at last secured a needed and nobly earned rest. He is now on his way to Whipple Barracks, A.T., where he will remain a few days to pack up; and then he will proceed to his new post.

I have already mentioned his fatherly kindness to the Indians in all their tediousness and childishness. It touched me a good deal. Equally noticeable is his fondness for children. In the busiest and most discouraging hours of the campaign he would unbend his eyebrows for a little romp with Laura, Major Roberts' lovely three-year-old, who thinks the world of the tall old warrior who will drop the Apache renegades for a space to toss her in his arms. With cheerful unconventionality she calls him "Crookie," and has no compunctions about assailing him at any point. Her bugaboo is the goat, which she holds in holy horror. When the General had the misfortune to singe his beard and eyebrows the other day, Laura set up a wail of distress and ran to her mother, crying, "I don't like Crookie any more — he looks like a billy-goat!" Ever since that catastrophe she has refused to sit next to him at table. She bowled me over the other day by exclaiming, when the General wouldn't tell her something: "Crookie, you're an old bump on a log!" Verily, childhood, like death, is no respecter of persons.

IF PROVIDENCE had particularly laid itself out to back up what I have said about Arizona economizers of the truth and the way Apache war news has been propagated, it couldn't have done much better than circumstance has during the last few days. The other day I noticed in a "Frisco" paper a long special from Tombstone, relating that "the celebrated scout Frank Leslie, better known as Buckskin Frank," had just arrived. He "has been for many months chief of scouts, is in General Crook's confidence, and gives the first authentic account of the escape of Geronimo." Then followed a lot of inaccurate and foolish though harmless romancing. The real news had been pub-

lished in the same paper several days before, and the above was, of course, merely a dodge of the alleged celebrity to advertise himself. There is a lot of such stuff sent out over the country for no other end than the glorification of some Arizona pillar of the saloon.

This man Leslie is a peculiar case, one of a class not infrequently met on the frontier — apparently well educated, gentlemanly and liked by all who know him; with as much sand as the country he ranges — but a novelist who can make a little truth cover a large area. As much fact as you could pick up on a pin point would last him a year. But there is one thing about it, his prevarications are all harmless. He never lies to hurt anybody — least of all to hurt Frank Leslie. It is the prime ambition of his existence to figure as a scout, and a scout he will be, if wild-cat dispatches from Tombstone can make him one. He was for a few weeks connected with Captain Crawford's command, hunting Geronimo, but was directly discharged for his inability to tell an Indian trail from a box of flea-powder. Therein lies his claim to distinction as a celebrated scout. But though he is no scout, he is no dude. He has killed two men, under circumstances of Arizona propriety, is a fine shot, and can ride farther and harder in a day than any other white man you could rake up with a fine-toothed comb. As to his "enjoying General Crook's confidence," you should have heard the quiet old General laugh when I showed him that dispatch.

By contrast, a sketch of the career of a real scout, the modest Frank Bennett, will not be found uninteresting. Mr. Bennett was born in Minnesota, where his father was for eight years register of the United States Land Office. In 1870 young Bennett struck out for the wild West, going to the Indian Territory as a scout under Lieutenant Colonel Lewis (who was killed in 1876 by the Sioux) and serving under him during the Cheyenne war. He was present at the fight which the gallant Rucker had with the famous Black Kettle and his band. Out here his campaigning came near being summarily ended. Nearly opposite the little town of Grenada, one day, the cavalry horses became stampeded and broke pellmell through the tents. The wives of Lieutenant Compton and Captain Chaffee were in one tent which was knocked down, and Bennett sprang to it just as a band of the terrified horses were about to trample it under foot. Seizing a pole he split the onset, and the animals passed on either side of the tent without injuring the ladies. But a heavy stake pin, flying at the end of a lariat, struck Bennett on the head, and he was stretched senseless on the ground. Taken to Fort Lyons, he lay there for nine weeks at the point of death. For six weeks he could not even turn over in bed. He remained home a year. An ugly hole above his left ear still remains as a reminder of his chivalrous deed.

Fully himself again, Bennett once more turned his face westward, making the trip via La Junta to Camp Verde in northern Arizona on horseback and landing in Prescott. He was there when the Chiricahuas first made themselves felt. Prescott was then about the jumping-off place. Everything had to be freighted in from the East or from the coast. Beans were sixteen cents a pound, bacon fifty cents, and flour twenty-eight to thirty dollars per hundredweight.

After many creditable experiences Bennett, in July of 1881, took up the trail after Nanay's band, which, sneaking up from Mexico, had seriously wounded two of the army packers. It was a hot and bloody chase and the hostiles were, during part of the time, travelling a hundred miles a day and never stopping to build a fire. In the forty-one days of pursuit Bennett had many running fights, one lasting for sixteen miles, killed a number of the renegades, captured many of their effects, and travelled one thousand, two hundred and forty-seven miles. When he turned the trail over to Captain Parker and went to Fort Wingate, he arrived with but nineteen of the fifty-two pack and saddle animals with which he had started the chase. All the rest had worn themselves out and had to be shot.

Among the noteworthy persons I have met here is Thomas Moore, nominally Chief Packer of the Department of the Missouri, but in fact Master of Transportation of the whole Army of the United States. He has an odd,

kindly, homely face, twinkling gray eyes, and a droll turn
of conversation. He is a man of clear, original and often
deep ideas. If there is any creed of universal popular ac-
ceptance, it is that the mule, and particularly the army
mule, can't be properly engineered without a club and
plenty of profanity. But here is a man who has more to do
with army mules than anyone else in the country, a man
who never swears at anything, and who discharges any
employee whom he catches raining blows and profanity
upon one of the long-eared train.

"The mule," Moore said to me, "has never been done
justice. It is fashionable to disparage him. People do so
without knowing anything about the subject. God made
the mule on purpose. The horse was designed for something
more than a servant to man. God saw that man needed a
true body servant, so He built the mule. Almost as soon
as he is able to walk the mule begins to be used, and his
tireless service ends only when he is dead. Even then he
serves a purpose, and is valued for his hide. He is always
faithful and reliable. He understands his work, does it as
few men do theirs. The idea that he must be cursed and
clubbed to work is pure idiocy. He does best with kind
treatment. Kick? Yes, he has a bad reputation as a kicker,
but that arises mostly from faulty handling. I am in less
danger of being kicked when among mules than when
among horses. A man accustomed to handling horses would
be in less danger among them than among mules. A green-
horn, unused to either, would be in more danger among
horses than among mules."

In striking contrast to Moore is another old character
here — the only swearer I ever heard who interlarded his
syllables with oaths. "Obligation?" he will thunder. "God

damn you, sir, I'm under no damned obli-by-God-gation to you, sir, God damn you, sir!"

. . . .

Coming out here I brought along a pair of boots with blue tops, expecting to do considerable riding. The plaguey things were as sawful on the ankle as if someone had been polishing me with a rasp. So I took them down to the Apache camp one day while the whole outfit was there playing coon-can, and made commercial overtures. Upon one young Chiricahua who sported a fine pair of pug-nosed moccasins I impressed the gorgeous advantages of those boots — particularly the blue tops. Becoming infatuated with them, he pulled off a moccasin and inserted his toes into the boot. I gave up the trade at once, for when his toes touched bottom his heel was still half-way up the leg. He was no tenderfoot, however. Remarking that the boot was "dam not long," he stamped and pulled and tugged and wrestled. He sweated and fumed and grew a fine meerschaum color in the face, but he kept at that boot for half an hour — and when at last he got it on, his big toe bulged out over the end of the sole. Nevertheless he was happy. Thereupon he went through the same circus with the other foot, handed me his moccasins, and stamped off as happy as a dog with two tails. Those boots would have caused the funeral of any other man save an Apache scout long before this, but a little thing like that won't disturb him a bit. You see, all these scouts are travelling immense distances daily over the roughest country in the world, with nothing between their soles and the rocks but a thin moccasin, and their feet become like the nether millstone of a politician's conscience. I had a curious illustration of this at the hospital the other day. When the Mexicans attacked Captain Crawford's force in Sonora last January, they first fired into the camp, shooting one of the scouts through both hips, and doing him the utmost damage that can be done a man. The poor devil had six holes in him, all made by one bullet. When I went to the hospital to see him he was feeling pretty blue, apparently, and was singing a doleful ululation to the earth-mother, the sun, the winds, and various spare entities, calling on them to give him a new lease on life. He wouldn't pay any attention to visitors until he had finished. Then he cajoled a cigarette-paper and some tobacco from me, which he handled with Mexican dexterity. Then he sat up in bed, kicked his poor wasted legs from under the cover, turned up one calloused foot, and drew one of those torpedo parlor matches across his bare sole! A strip of sandpaper couldn't have been more effective. The match went off like a toy pistol. No use in expecting that sort of a foot to rebel at a little inhumanity on the part of a boot. That fellow, by the way, is fast getting well and was taken the other day to Fort Apache in a rough wagon.

You may be sure that while in the Territory I have not neglected the matter of relics. Not to mention canes of the dried stalk of the century plant, beans from the mezquite, a bushel box of various cacti from the savage recesses of Apache Pass, a bundle of the beautiful red manzanita wood, and such inferior trophies, I got some mementos which were really worth while. When the captives came up from the Cañon de los Embudos, I began to cultivate them at once. Chihuahua, the chief, cottoned to me and my two-bit cigars, and the friendliest relations were soon established between us. He is a superb-looking Indian, smart as cayenne, and "the wildest-mannered man that ever scuttled ship or cut a throat." I used to go down after supper to their camp, a mile from the fort, and sit with them around their campfires till way into the night, studying their ways and talking as best we could, the Spanish on both sides being very meek. It was a striking place for an evening loaf, down among savages of the bloodiest reputation in our land, and not another white skin in sight. It did seem a little lonely sometimes, but I had the utmost confidence in Chihuahua, and I think the old fellow conceived a genuine affection for me. At any rate, when they left for Florida, he came riding around to find me, with his bright seven-year-old perched behind him, got off, embraced me, and said goodbye in as cordial a way as it was ever said. He gave me the big silver disc he wore at his throat, and at my special request, the tattered yellow handkerchief which he had worn as a headdress during most of the campaign. From Keowtennay, the most famous of the friendly Apaches, I secured a valuable necklace of the peculiar Apache style. From Ulzanna, the bloodiest of raiders, I got an Apache flute. Old Nanay, the right hand of Victorio, contributed to my collection his fine buckskin tobacco pouch.

CHAPTER **VIII**

AMONG THE HUMOROUS paragraphs interjected among the
red pages of the Apache campaign one has stood pre-
eminent — the cry of the cowboy howling to be let at 'em.
The exuberant knight of the lariat has had to keep his
friends implored to hold him down lest he avalanche himself upon the hostiles and at one fell swipe expunge the
Apache race. By emphasis of profanity and iteration he has
actually caused some good people to yearn for the formation of cowboy companies, in faith that thus the problem
should be solved instanter, and the proposition has even
been gravely wired to Washington.

The cowboy is a first rate fellow. I haven't a word to say

against him, but have, *per contra*, the memory of many a kindness at his hands. He's rough, but for that the range he rides is more to blame than he. The primmest of us all would lose the refined gloss under like circumstances. He has manly virtues not a few, and they are as virile as his vices. To damn him by wholesale is not only unjust but silly. As an Indian fighter, however, he is a rank failure. He has neither the experience nor the disposition to trail; and if it ever comes to a fight he must gallop madly about at a salutary distance, whoop and swing his hat, and promulgate his six-shooter or Winchester — to the mortal peril of the circumambient air, but not of anything else in particular. If you deduce thereby that he is a coward, you were never so badly fooled in your life. Probably no class of men is more absolutely contemptuous of death. He will pluck the grim old reaper by the beard at any time and never twitch an eyelid. But he wants to see the deal in any game in which he takes a hand. In the bar-room broil, where the friendly glass spills an ugly word, where the word is echoed by a blow and the blow gets answer in the instant flash of twenty revolvers — there the cowboy is at home. Untrembling as the rocks, you shall see him face the murderous music of the forty-fours, his own barking back adequate reply. Sieve him with bullet holes and still he will bring down his man. There is a recreation which he comprehends, and comprehending, you will find him clear grit to the last flutter of his heart.

But it is "the danger we know not of" which makes cowards of us all. The cowboy knows nothing of Indians. It isn't his business. Unflinchingly as he will face the danger that he can *see*, when it comes to fighting an invisible, an unknown and mysterious foe, he "isn't there." I don't blame him — it shows his width between the eyes. To gallop or creep through a waste so bleak, so barren and so desolate that it oppresses the senses, amid a silence heavy enough to break the heart, seeing no sign of life, yet ever on the nettles of consciousness that any innocent bunch of bear-grass, any cactus rosette, any lonely rock, may unwarning spit out its puff of sudden smoke to carry a leaden message to your heart — isn't it enough to make anyone a bit loose at the knees? The man whose heart doesn't feel now and then in this warfare as though all the props had been kicked from under it — he isn't a hero. He is either an ignorant fool or a crazy one. No, bravery alone is not enough. It takes experience, and that the cowboy has not.

As for discipline — why, discipline him and he would be no longer a cowboy. His absolute independence and individuality are himself. If it will amuse anyone to pick up cowboys and heave them at the meteoric Apache, the target won't complain if the missile doesn't. No one will get hurt — save the cowboys perforated by their brethren — and there will be as much fun as there isn't gore. But don't ask the government to subsidize the puncher. That would be crowding the mourners.

In illustration of how the cowpuncher fares when his wits are matched against those of the crafty Apache, let me relate a few short chapters of true but unwritten history.

Last October when Ulzanna and his band were raiding through New Mexico and Arizona, hard pushed by Crook's efficient captains, it came to pass one day that the old men and children of the band, with four or five bucks who could fight, swept down on White's rancho, twenty-five miles south of Fort Bowie. Camping in the open plain, half a mile from the house and in full view of it, they killed two or three beeves, roasted them, ate all they could hold and packed all they could carry. In the night they flitted silently away, unmolested. Inside the strong stockade of that ranch-house were twenty-five or thirty cowboys, weighed down with Winchesters and six-shooters. Did they open fire on the superannuated foe? Nary open. *They* hadn't lost any Indians!

Ulzanna and his band holed up in the Chiricahua mountains, whence they tried twice to break across the San Simon valley to Stein's Peak range on the northeast; but were each time deterred by troops "laying for" them. At last they made a night dash to the westward, across the Sulphur Springs valley. Their stock was on its last legs, and while the rest rode across the valley, three or four

69

bucks went to the Sulphur Springs rancho for fresh mounts. There were several punchers sleeping in the house that night, and the strong high stockade which protected the horses was securely locked and barred. The Chiricahuas borrowed an axe from the woodpile, chopped down enough palisades, took all the horses and vanished. The cowboys did not fire a shot — indeed, I believe they knew nothing of the affair until morning. To one who has wooed sleep under the raucous Niagara of a cowboy's snore, this seems highly plausible.

Ponies, lariats and all, Captain Crawford chased the re-mounted renegades through the Mule and Dragoon mountains. Then they whipped square to the left and made for the Chiricahua peaks again, with Crawford still hanging on their trail. The day after they got back to this range he found the spot where, hard run and with failing stock, they had stabbed every one of their animals to death and scattered on foot amid the rocks. Then he thought he had a line on them, sure. Just at this time the cowboys of the San Simon valley were preparing for the fall round-up and had gathered in force at a rancho near the mouth of Whitetail Cañon, with twenty-five or thirty prime ponies nicely shod and ready for the fun. They were warned that the hostiles had been seen on the neighboring peaks that day and that it would be horse sense to put their ponies in the stout corral that night. But no, they wouldn't have it so. They'd like to see any blankety-blank Indians get away with any of *their* livestock. So they insisted on picketing their ponies out on the grass while themselves snored conscientiously inside the house. When they awoke next morning and rubbed their confident eyes, every last pony was gone, lariat and all. Crawford's tremendous pursuit found only the swift trail of these fresh horses, sweeping far down into the safety of Sonora. It's a lucky thing the cowboys slept inside that night. Had they camped out beside the ponies, the raiders might have carried *them* off.

These are fair samples of the fashion in which the cowboy emerges from the diminutive extremity of the cornucopia when he has to deal with the lightning movements and matchless cunning of the Apache.

Thus much for the puncher. Commoner than he and infinitely more jawsome is the Territorial terror — the bad man from Sinville. When he looms above the horizon, the inadequate steer-steerer pales his ineffectual fires. I can give you no better diagram of him than by relating a little episode of actual occurrence.

On the eve of Crook's departure for the Sierra Madres in the Apache campaign of '83 one of those companies of citizens was organized in Tombstone to quench all Apachedom. They were of the class of Arizonans who make the noise. There are lots of good people in this Territory, but they are not the talkers. I forget the official name of the cohort but the current name among disinterested outsiders was "The Tombstone Toughs," and they were going to wind up the war in a week. Going to the line in hay wagons — it *is* hard to carry a jug in the saddle — they swooped upon the Mexican custom-house and explained that they were bound for the Sierra Madres to obliterate the hostiles. To their infinite disgust, the Mexican officials were delighted with the idea. Here was a pretty how-de-do, a fine state of things. What! Were they not only to be allowed but fairly encouraged to beard the lion in his lair? It was simply murderous! One of them was heard to remark: "Wonder why the hell they don't stop us?" The Toughs dawdled around the line until it became hideously plain that no one would stop them — and then went home.

71

Their next proposition was to march on the reservation and butcher the eight thousand Apaches peacefully farming there — men, women, and children. A horrid proposition, truly, in the eyes of all decent folk, eastern or Arizonan; but still a very popular one in this Territory. The Tombstone Toughs, superbly mounted, galloped north and camped displayfully some nine miles from Wilcox, where Crook was then preparing to make his personal expedition into Sonora. That was the reason why the avengers stopped near Willcox. They also took care that Crook should know of their coming. But, somehow, the quiet old soldier refused to be stampeded. Nay, he wouldn't send out so much as a boy with a pea-shooter to quell the Gory Exterminators. Soon weary of waiting to be collared, they invaded Willcox, retailing their plan to make a grease spot of the reservation. And still "damned old Crook" refused to pay any attention to them. No one stuck so much as a straw in their way. Cursing the bloodthirsty heartlessness of the army, the Toughs loped away at last to Fort Thomas. Crook, the sly old fox, had already telegraphed the commanding officer there to treat them with perfect courtesy and unconcern, and the order was carried out to the letter. There was now but one desperate alternative left the Toughs. They spurred away toward the reservation.

Official word was sent the Indians that while there was really no danger, it might be well to keep one eye peeled. They did. The Apache is not one of those to wait for a kick. So it befell that every possible approach to their homes was guarded. You might have ridden by those hills a hundred times and never suspected danger, but it is gospel that if the Toughs had been one hundred companies instead of one, they would have never got through alive. They didn't know this and they didn't need to. It would have been a wild waste of wind to tell them. They rode to within a day's march of the boundary hills, camped until their ginspiration gave out — and then tore home. Not having so much as seen the reservation, they publicly reported that they had been up there, looked things over and found all was perfectly satisfactory. The reservation Indians were working hard and honestly, and it would really be wrong to kill them!

Thus ended the gory career of the Tombstone Toughs. It reminds one of that famous campaign:

> "The noble Duke of York,
>   He had ten thousand men,
> He marched them up a hill one day,
>   Then — marched them down again!"

CHAPTER **IX**

THE DETAILED STORY of one expedition among many of this campaign gives an idea of just how easy it is to run down the wild raiders. I would like to see about two hundred newspaper men whom I could mention forced to join such an expedition. Their brains might then get rid of a little of their present military flatulence.

The command left Fort Bowie July 17, 1885. It was composed as follows: Captain Wirt Davis, Fourth Cavalry; Lieutenant Erwin, Fourth Cavalry; two companies (a hundred and two men) of White Mountain, San Carlos and Chiricahua Apache scouts, commanded by First Lieutenant M. W. Day, Ninth Cavalry, Second Lieutenant Robert D.

Walsh, Fourth Cavalry, and Roberts and Leslie, Chiefs of
Scouts; Assistant Surgeon H. P. Birmingham; and two pack
trains. Reaching Lang's ranch (in the very southwestern
corner of New Mexico) on the twelfth, they were joined by
thirty-eight men of the Fourth Cavalry. They left Lang's
the following day, crossed the line into Mexico and marching via the Sierra Media and Dos Carretas Creek (Chihuahua), Bavispe, Baserac and Guachineva (Sonora), arrived
at Huépere Creek, a hundred and seven miles from Lang's,
on the nineteenth. Here they intended to rest, but at dusk
on the twentieth a Mexican mail carrier brought word
from the Prefect of Montezuma District that the citizens of

Oposura had followed eighty or a hundred Apaches — mostly women and children — from near the Sonora River, where they had been depredating, westward toward the Teres mountains, Sonora. Upon receipt of this news, Captain Davis and his command left camp at 5:20 the following morning, and marched thirty-three miles across the Huépere, Madera and Oputo mountains, and camped at 6:00 P.M. six miles north of Oputo. The Presidente of Oputo informed them that the hostiles had that day fired upon the citizens fifteen miles north, and that twenty-five or thirty citizens had started in pursuit. These pursuers reached Captain Davis' camp at sunset and told him that the hostiles had killed a beef and taken it into the La Joya mountains. As soon as it became dark he sent out six scouts to locate the hostile camp, and next morning marched down the Bavispe River and camped in a concealed position a mile below Oputo. Two of the six scouts came back to him at six o'clock on the evening of the twenty-second, and said that by watching the squaws out gathering cactus, they had located the camp on the highest peak of the La Joya mountains. At midnight Captain Davis left his pack train under guard, and with two days' rations marched across very rough country until dawn, which found him nine miles north of Oputo. Here the horses were tied to trees, and all the men concealed themselves in the timber. In the afternoon all the scouts were sent out on foot through the arroyos and mesquite thickets to join the four who had remained to watch the hostile camp. At 7 P.M. Davis dismounted his cavalry and went with them up the mountain. By daylight the command had completely surrounded the hostile camp only to find, with the light of day, that in spite of the utmost precaution, the enemy had noiselessly decamped! Fragments of dresses found in the deserted camp were recognized by scouts as belonging to women of Geronimo's band.

Ascertaining the direction taken by the hostiles and sending a scout back for the pack train, Davis quietly moved his force down to the Bavispe River and camped, hidden in the cane-breaks and timber, near the mouth of the San Juan, where he was joined by the pack train. The scouts informed him that there was a big spring on the eastern slope of the La Joyas, where the renegades often stopped for six or seven days to roast mescal, abundant there. He sent eighty-six of his best scouts with five days' short rations into the La Joyas to surprise the hostiles or follow their trail toward Huépere Creek, where he would join them on August first. With the rest of his command he marched down to Bavispe and across the mountains to Huépere Creek, ten miles southeast of Guachineva, arriving there on schedule and finding his scouts with good news. On the twenty-eighth of July, Bi-er-ley, first sergeant of Walsh's scouts, had gone into the La Joyas with a few scouts and had ambushed four hostiles, killing two and capturing four horses, three saddles, bridles and blankets.

The trail of the hostiles now passed three miles west of Huépere, bearing south towards the Sierra Madres. On the second of August, Davis sent Lieutenant Day and Chief of Scouts Roberts with seventy-eight picked scouts and all the rations that could be spared, out on the trail, telling them as soon as the pack train returned from Lang's he would proceed with the balance of the command to Nacori. Davis kept in camp near Huépere with Lieutenant Walsh and twenty-four scouts; and on August third he sent Lieutenant Erwin with a detachment of cavalry and the two pack trains to Lang's for forty days' rations. Pending the return of the pack train he sent Walsh and Leslie out several times to look for trails, thinking that Chihuahua's band — which had been attacked by Captain Crawford's scouts June twenty-third — might move toward the Sierra Madres in the same general direction which Geronimo had taken. General D. M. Guerra with five hundred Mexican cavalry had arrived at Bavispe about August first, either marching against the Yaquis or to protect Sonora against the hostiles. He marched within five or six miles of Davis but they did not meet.

On the afternoon of August seventh, Lieutenant Day and his scouts surprised Geronimo's camp about thirty miles north-northeast of Nacori, killed three bucks, one squaw, one boy and a child, besides capturing fifteen squaws and children, thirteen horses and mules, the blankets, saddles and whole camp outfit.

On August fourteenth, the pack animals returned loaded from Lang's, and on the fifteenth Davis and his command started for Nacori, taking part of one pack train loaded with rations. Arriving at Bacadehuachi the same day after a march of thirty-one miles, they found Lieutenant Huse with Company C, Fourth Cavalry, and some Chiricahua prisoners from Captain Crawford. Next day the prisoners were all sent to Fort Bowie with Huse, and Davis sent for Lieutenant Day and his scouts and directed Lieutenant Erwin to join him with the balance of the command and the pack train which had been left at Babi rancho. August twentieth the whole command camped at Ojo Caliente and rested for three days. Captain Crawford had gone into the Sierra Madres in pursuit of Geronimo's scattered band.

Learning from the Prefect of Oposura that twenty or twenty-five hostiles were in the mountains between Oposura and Tepache, Davis started at once, August twenty-third, in pursuit. Crossing the Huasivas and Oposura mountains, and passing through the towns of Granadas and Huasivas, the command, on the twenty-sixth, arrived at Toni-babi, in the mountains nine miles east of Oposura. A vaquero sent out by the Presidente of Granadas showed them the trail made by twelve or fifteen hostiles the day before. After following this trail a short distance with a few scouts, Davis found that the hostiles were going slowly. He decided to leave his pack train at Toni-babi, take a few mules, travel all night and lie concealed by day until he surprised the hostiles, who were headed toward the Espinosa [Espinazo?] del Diablo, the roughest region in all Mexico. That night Captain Davis received a note from General Guerra, asking a meeting in the morning. Next morning Guerra came over with his officers and an escort, all neatly uniformed. He said his troops had had a fight on July twenty-fifth with the hostiles Davis was pursuing, and that one hostile and two Mexicans had been killed. He wanted some of Davis' scouts to go with him as trailers, but they declined. (I'd like some hydrophobic journals to note this Mexican testimony to the value of the Apache scouts.)

Davis again took up the trail and went to the scene of the fight between the Mexicans and the renegades, thence to the top of Mount Salitral, twenty miles southeast of Tepache, and about opposite the junction of the Haros and Bavispe rivers. Here the hostiles, seeing that they were closely pursued, had taken their knives and killed their stock — sixteen horses and mules, besides eleven which they had similarly killed at scattered points along the trail. Here the scouts got three saddles, five blankets, one horse and one mule, the latter slightly wounded. It was now impossible to pick up the trail beyond this point, as after killing their stock the hostiles had scattered on foot, and

79

their footprints had been obliterated by a heavy rain that had since fallen. Davis camped at Palmiramenes, east of Mt. Salitral, and stayed there the next day, August thirty-first. The scouting party which he sent around the mountain could find no trace of the scattered hostiles. From the beds which were found on top of the mountain the scouts learned that the band they were then pursuing was Chihuahua's, and consisted of one or two boys, one squaw and twelve bucks.

Thinking that the band would finally leave Sonora and raid into Chihuahua via the Teres mountains, Davis decided to march between these mountains and Nacosari. He started September first, moved slowly and cautiously toward the Bavispe River, and marched up that stream through Granadas and Huasivas, camping September sixth in an arroyo ten miles north of Huasivas. Next day Lieutenant Cole arrived from Huépere with rations and commissary funds and was sent back with the pack train on the ninth to Lang's ranch. On the twelfth Davis started out again by way of Oputo and camped next day in the Cañon de los Huedigos, sixteen miles north-northeast of Oputo. The cañon was deep, full of large trees (huedigos) and dense undergrowth, and afforded a fine place of concealment for the troops. There was water and grass in the side cañons, so the horses could graze unseen. Davis had written General Guerra to have the Mexican cavalry at Cumpas and Nacosari keep a sharp lookout, as the dismounted hostiles were apt to sneak over there and steal mules and horses.

On the fourteenth Davis sent out Lieutenant Day and his company of scouts northward toward Dos Pilores, on the Bavispe River, to see if he could find any trails leading east. He also dispatched parties of Lieutenant Walsh's scouts westward on a similar mission. On the eighteenth Lieutenant Day returned, having found no trails. On the same day Davis received a note from P. G. Hatcher of the American Ranch, between Nacosari and Cumpas, stating that on the night of the fourteenth the hostiles had stolen fourteen horses and mules from his ranch. On the nineteenth Davis started for Nacosari. After marching four or five miles he found concealed in a ravine a man and a woman, Americans from Tombstone on their way from Nacosari to some mines in the Nacosari mountains. On the preceding afternoon their party — four men and the woman — had been attacked by Apaches. One American was killed and all their burros seized. Taking the man and woman, Davis camped immediately in the mountains at Nogalitos Spring, in concealment. In the afternoon he left Lieutenant Erwin there with the cavalry, eighteen scouts and a pack train, and with eighty-four scouts and a pack train with twenty days' rations, pushed forward on the trail. They found and buried the dead American, but could discover no trace of the two who had run away. Near the dead man were four empty shotgun cartridges. The brave woman, when the man was shot down, had snatched the shotgun and scattered four loads of buckshot at the Indians, while her two valiant countrymen were running for dear life and leaving her to shift for herself. But she was equal to the occasion. Under fire from the hostiles she went up to the dead man's body, snatched his belt full of cartridges and his Winchester, and retreated in good order. When Captain Davis found her and the one man who had stood by her, she had the cartridge belt around her waist, the shotgun in one hand, and the Winchester in the other. Davis thinks one of the hostiles is salted yet with some of the lead from this heroine's gun. If the blowhard fraternity of Arizona could be vaccinated from Mrs. Belle Davis, we might hear of their killing an occasional Apache.

Pursuing the trail, apparently made by twenty or twenty-five Indians, and following it day and night, the command arrived at noon on the twenty-second in a rugged cañon near the summit of the Teres mountains. The hostiles were travelling rapidly and leaving a guard behind to watch for pursuers. Davis sent out Sergeant Cooley (an Apache in Day's command) with nineteen picked scouts and several field-glasses to keep two or three men ahead, travel slowly and cautiously off the trail and locate the hostiles, who were evidently not far ahead. Davis himself was to follow in two or three hours with the rest of the command. He started at 3 P.M., having directed packer Patrick to follow with the pack train at 4, but to stop if he heard firing. Davis had marched a mile and a half when he heard five rifle shots three or four miles ahead, and apparently on the trail. He hurried his scouts ahead to the firing, and just before sunset they overtook and speedily routed the Indians, who fled into the mountains. It seems that Cooley had struck the rear guard of the hostiles and captured their horses, after which he imprudently pushed two sergeants ahead on their trail. On a ridge covered with dense chapparal, about a mile from where they had captured the horses, the two sergeants literally walked into an ambush which the fleeing hostiles had left. One sergeant, Cooley's brother, was killed *within ten feet* of the man who shot him. That will give you an idea of the skill of the Apache ambush. The other sergeant escaped. In the ensuing fight, Davis' scouts, stripping for the fray according to their custom, showed great spirit. One of them was slightly wounded in the thigh. One hostile was killed, and one or two others must have been wounded, for stained bandages and considerable blood were found on the trail the next day.

The command camped after dark on the scene of the battle. Next morning (September twenty-third), after burying the dead sergeant, they resumed the pursuit, going through the Teres mountains, across the Bavispe River, and northeastward toward Chihuahua. On the twenty-fifth Davis sent a courier to Lieutenant Erwin at Nogalitos, to go with his men to Dos Carretas Creek, Chihuahua. He also sent a message through the Presidente of Bavispe to Captain Crawford, recounting the fight in the Teres mountains, the direction the fugitives had taken, and Davis' belief that they had all left Sonora and gone over into Chihuahua. The trail which Davis followed over steep mountains and across savage cañons debouched on Janos plains, six or seven miles north of Dos Carretas Creek. The hostiles, though now well mounted, were not over four hours ahead of the pursuers. As soon as the Apaches reached the plain they set out at a gallop and, having gone eight or ten miles thus nearly due east, scattered in all directions. At eight o'clock that night, September twenty-fifth, Davis camped on Dos Carretas Creek. Just before dawn on the twenty-sixth, Lieutenant Elliot arrived with fifty scouts from Captain Crawford, who was camped on the creek four or five miles above Davis and had received the latter's note at midnight. As the command started out toward the Sierra Media to cut the hostile trail, Crawford joined them. After much time and labor in following the trail of single horses, they struck the main trail of the Indians in the Raton mountains, ten miles north of where the fugitives had scattered. From here Davis sent a courier to Lang's with a dispatch advising General Crook that the fugitives were headed toward Guadalupe Cañon. The trail now led four or five miles into the plain and thence back again into the

83

Ratons. On the twenty-seventh Lieutenant Elliott got back from the Sierra Media and rejoined Davis and Crawford, and the whole command, moving as rapidly as possible, reached Guadalupe Cañon the next day. The Apaches had crossed the cañon in the morning, about five miles above the cavalry command stationed there. Before daylight next morning, Captain Martin, Fourth Cavalry, with Troop H and some scouts, started in pursuit.

Davis' scouts had now followed the hostile trail rapidly for two hundred and seventy miles. Twenty or thirty of the fugitives were nearly exhausted and many more had torn moccasins and lacerated feet. Captain Crawford and his scouts were comparatively fresh; so Davis sent them on the trail, and himself returned to Fort Bowie, after an absence of ninety days. In that ninety days the command

had covered between nine hundred and a thousand miles, not counting the great distances covered by detachments and scouting parties. "But miles," very sensibly says Captain Davis, "do not convey a correct idea of the work done. The country is rough and rugged beyond description. The heat, particularly above Oposura, Tepache and the Bavispe River, was intense and stifling. To cap the climax of our discomfort, heavy rainstorms in August and September drenched the command and everything it had. Mosquitos and other insects tortured us at night; and by day we were fully occupied in trying to find and circumvent the wily foe. In such heat the diet of bacon, beans and hastily-cooked bread lost its charm. But the hardships were cheerfully borne by all. The scouts behaved zealously and did effective service through the whole campaign."

Captain Crawford, Third Cavalry, who took up the trail of the Apaches, enlisted his battalion of Chiricahua and White Mountain Apaches at the reservation on November 9, 1885, and a month later crossed the Mexican line in pursuit of Geronimo and his renegades. Crawford was personally acquainted with all the hostiles and all the scouts. He was not only an ideal Indian fighter but an ideal man. Yet the chief attention paid by the American press to his assassination by Mexican troops last January (1886 — T. L. F.) seems to lie in the line of apology for the assassins. At this date, three months after the tragedy, Lieutenant Maus' extemely accurate and detailed report has never been published, the meager and unworkmanlike alleged epitome of it giving but a feeble idea of its force. I have taken the verbatim statements of the men directly concerned in the affair — Lieutenant Maus and Lieutenant Shipp — and herewith present them.

The troops had had an incredibly tedious chase before they located the camp of the hostiles, or "bronchos," amid the rocks of a ridge near the Haros River in Sonora, nearly two hundred miles south of the line of New Mexico. First Lieutenant Marion P. Maus, First Infantry, upon whom the command devolved at Crawford's death, is a faithful, intelligent, and honorable officer. He says:

"Just before daybreak on the tenth we surprised the broncho camp. We were trying to surround it quietly, but that is a tamalpais [malpais? — T. L. F.] country and a few rolling stones set their burros to braying. The hostiles, taking the alarm, hid in the rocks and opened fire on us. Our scouts responded. It was still perfectly dark so that we could not see their camp and were guided only by the flash of a rifle here and there. No one was hurt on our side, but we found several pools of blood in the hostile camps.

The hostiles escaped into the mountains before daylight. We got their whole camp outfit — blankets, dried meat, roasted mescal, etc., to the amount of several wagon-loads — with thirty horses and mules. We had been marching steadily since 11 A.M. the day before, and were worn out. Captain Crawford sent back for his pack-train of eleven mules, and we camped just beyond the broncho camp to rest. Next morning, the eleventh, we were awakened about daybreak by our scouts, who called out that Mexican soldiers were coming. As nearly as I can fix the time, it was just about daybreak. I could recognize a person probably one hundred yards away. Immediately upon this alarm by our scouts, a severe fire was opened by the Mexicans. Lieutenant Shipp and I, with Mr. Horn, the chief of scouts, ran out to stop the attack. The firing (by the Mexicans) was so severe as to stop us before we got to where our scouts were (some sixty yards away), and we sought shelter. The Mexicans had taken a high position about two hundred yards north and were firing down into us. Our scouts called out in broken English who we were, and Horn and I kept calling in Spanish, We are American soldiers! Don't shoot! We are friends! All of us kept shouting, thinking that the Mexicans had attacked us by mistake. We didn't wish to kill them, supposing that they were friends and hadn't recognized us. At our command our scouts did not fire at all until the Mexicans had been shooting about ten minutes. Even then there were but a few shots and these were from scouts so far away we couldn't stop them. Our command being concealed in Indian fashion, the Mexicans had no idea how many we were, and by their initial actions showed that they thought we were very weak numerically. Please remember that important point. They were so near and we were calling so loudly and so constantly that at last they stopped, after at least fifteen or twenty minutes of firing. When the firing ceased, a party of nine of them came out directly to where we were, and fourteen or fifteen more circled around farther to our front and right, while a third party, farther off, moved toward our right flank to get possession of a high point that commanded our position. The nine Mexicans of the first party mentioned came to within thirty yards of where our scouts were in the rocks. Captain Crawford and I, from different points in the rocks, walked out to talk with them. I was within six feet of the Mexican Captain, and said to him in Spanish: Don't you see we are American soldiers? Look at my uniform and the captain's. He looked very nervous and frightened, and with another man kept saying: *Sí! Sí! Sí! Sí! No Tires! No Tires!'* (Don't shoot!)

It was plain enough why he was nervous. He was so close that he could see among the rocks the heads and rifles of fifty or sixty scouts. He kept edging off, continually saying *'No tires!'* and seemed to be trying to get behind a little hill. At this time Captain Crawford, seeing the necessity of having no shot fired on either side, called out to me: 'Maus, for God's sake go back there to the scouts and see that not a shot is fired!' I turned and passed in front of him, and had covered perhaps twenty of the thirty yards between us and the rocks when I heard a single shot behind me, followed by a heavy volley. That first shot was distinct to me above all else. It seemed like a death-knell. It flashed across me: 'Great God! These men are killing each other for nothing!' And on the heels of the thought came the volley. All of us sought cover. Crawford had come back from the open ground, got upon a rock, and turned back his face to the Mexicans, when he was shot through the forehead. The scouts say that that first single shot was the one that hit him."

Second Lieutenant W. E. Shipp, Tenth Cavalry, is a very tall, superbly built and blonde young officer, intelligent and straightforward. Like Maus, he is a West-Pointer. Of Crawford's death he says:

"When I first saw Captain Crawford, he was standing on top of a big rock about five feet high, where everyone could see his whole body. This was after the first firing had ceased. None of our white people had their weapons. There were about ten Mexicans close in front of us. Lieutenant Maus and Mr. Horn kept calling to them in Spanish: 'Don't shoot! We are American soldiers!' They kept answering, '*Sí! sí!*' (Yes, yes); but were all the time edging around till they got behind a tree. Then they opened fire without warning. Mr. Horn jumped down off his rock and grabbed his left arm. I asked him if he was hurt. He said yes. (The ball passed through the fleshy part of his arm.)

The Mexicans who shot at him were about twenty-five yards away. We were both in full view. I had on a brown hunting-coat, with the blue army trousers; Mr. Horn a civilian's suit. As soon as we had sheltered ourselves in the rocks, after Horn was shot, the scouts called out that Captain Crawford was killed. I went over to where he lay, about twenty yards away. He was on his back behind the rock upon which he had been standing. A silk handkerchief lay on the wound which was an inch above his left eyebrow. A piece of his brain as big as my two fingers lay on the rock. His hat was on the ground — a brown government field hat. He had on a full uniform. It was impossible to mistake him for an Indian."

Lieutenant Maus continued:

"Several of the Mexicans were still within easy hearing,

and Mr. Horn had been yelling to them all the time in Spanish. After the firing had ceased, and their attack had failed, I heard one of them calling: 'Come over and talk! Come over!' Mr. Horn started out toward them. I was going to call the courageous fellow back but instead followed him over to where some of them were lying. The Mexicans commenced a palaver and declared it was 'all a mistake,' they were 'very sorry,' 'what a great pity,' and so on. I was glad to have the murderous affair stop; and without reflection, in the hurry and excitement, accepted their explanations. They said we had killed their Captain, Corador, and also the next in command. The third in command, with whom I talked, was a sergeant named Santana Perez. There was another sergeant named Rancon. These two did the talking. They told me they were after the hostiles. I told them explicitly what we had done — how we had captured the camp and the animals of the hostiles — and they understood perfectly. They told me they had followed the trail of these Indians all the way from Chihuahua and had traveled nineteen days. This is not true. We had followed the hostile trail eight days from west to east, while the Mexicans came from the northeast, and never got nearer than a mile to the hostile trail. They did strike our trail at a point four or five miles from where they attacked us, and followed it in.

"They told me they were in a dreadful condition — worn out and without food. They asked me to give them something to eat, appealing piteously. Whenever you meet these Mexican volunteers they are always begging for something — usually food. They asked me to let our surgeon come over to keep their wounded from bleeding to death. If we would let him come over, and would send them half a dozen of the horses we had captured to carry their wounded, they would leave, as they wanted to go right home. I had many reasons for being anxious to get rid of them. Overtures of surrender had already been made the day before by Natchez, who had sent in two squaws, one after the other, to treat with us. I believe that, as we had captured everything of theirs save their persons and their arms, there was a good chance that the fugitives would have surrendered unconditionally, but they would never do it as long as the Mexicans were around, for they always suspect Mexican treachery. They have had abundant cause to in the past. Furthermore, our rations were nearly out and our ammunition almost exhausted. It was raining and the country, almost impassable for pack-trains, was hourly getting worse. When our pack-train would get in from Nacori was a matter of the greatest uncertainty. If the river got too high it couldn't reach us at all. Two of our wounded, Captain Crawford and a scout, had to be carried by hand, so we would have to move very slowly — and we were two hundred miles' march from the border.

"I promised the Mexicans I would do what I could for them. The doctor was not with us then, but got in that day, and as soon as he had attended to our wounded he went over and cared for theirs. That day, at their request, and to get rid of them, we exchanged papers. The one that Sergeant Perez gave me was to this effect: 'That they had met us unknowingly and had attacked us on the Haros River January eleventh and had fired upon us, not turning back; that it was dark, so that they could not see, and that they fought us by mistake.' My paper was to the effect that we had met them unknowingly and couldn't see perfectly when the first attack was made. (It was a little foggy then, though as I said, I could have recognized a person at a hundred yards — but when they killed Crawford it was perfectly light.) The doctor told me that our wounded could not be made any worse by moving them, so I commenced to make litters.

"Next morning, the twelfth, I sent over six of the captured horses to within a hundred yards of the Mexican camp and went on with my preparations for leaving. They refused to come down that hundred yards to get the horses but demanded that we bring them clear up. Mr. Horn and the interpreter who had taken the horses over refused to go any nearer, and told the Mexicans to talk with me.

"We were within half an hour of starting (about noon) when one of the scouts told me that several of the captured horses had wandered off to the hill beyond the Mexicans. I sent Concepción, one of our Mexican interpreters, over after the horses. When he got to where the Mexicans were they stopped him and asked him why we had not brought the horses clear up to them. He answered: 'Why didn't you come and take them when we brought them? I'm going after my horses — you go talk to Lieutenant Maus.' He was then going on, when the Mexican sergeant turned to his men and said: 'Keep this interpreter and don't let him escape. He shall die here with us.' Thereupon, Concepción sat down. They told him to call me over, and he did. I saw that he was in trouble — and I couldn't leave the poor old fellow there in a fix.

"Mr. Horn was wounded, and I was the only one left who could converse in Spanish. I went half-way across the ravine and said to them: 'Come down here if you want to talk to me. What have you to say?' They answered 'Come up here. Come up. We want to talk with you about those horses and see if we can't fix it up. Don't fear anything from us — we are friends.' They kept on protesting friendship, and I went up on the hill where about a dozen of them were standing. It was raining, and they proposed that we should go under a projecting rock a few yards off. As soon as we got around a little corner of the rocks, I saw the position. Full fifty Mexicans were lying up against the cliffs with their guns. They said: 'Sit down. We want to fix this business. We want those horses!' I said: 'I sent over those horses, why didn't you receive them?' They answered: 'You didn't bring them up to us.' Their manner was such as to make me think my position a ticklish one. They were a very tough-looking set, and acted very menacingly. I thought it best to take no notice of this and said in an off-hand way that I would go to my camp and send the horses. They said 'No! Send this man (Concepción) after them.' I saw the whole game and that they had me trapped. So I gave Concepción a note for Lieutenant Shipp, asking that he send over six of the captured horses. Concepción then spoke up and said to me: 'Captain, there are many of our horses over here. Let these people take them.' So I said to the Mexicans: 'Take six of the horses that are over here.' They declared there were none. Concepción said, rather angrily, that there were. I told the Mexicans to send out and see if he wasn't right. Some of them went out and brought back a roan mare, saying that there were no others. Then Concepción went to our camp and drove five of the captured horses over to me. The stock was pretty rough, but with the roan mare they had six, and that was all I had promised. The Mexicans however refused to accept them, saying: 'We won't have these. They're no use.' I said: 'Well, I'll go over to camp and send you six serviceable horses that you will take.' I got up and started to go, but they stopped me. How? They jumped in front of me, and all around me, a large number of them, saying, 'No! No!' in a menacing manner. I said: 'Do you mean to tell me that

I can't leave here and go to my own camp?' They told me very plainly that that was just what they meant. Then they commenced to ask me what right I had in Mexico, what papers I had, etc. I had no papers. Captain Crawford had had the papers but they were with the pack-train near Nacori. I told them that they should know that I had a right to be there, that under the existing treaty the troops of either nation could cross the line in pursuit of the hostiles, and that as Mexican soldiers they must know this fact. They told me they knew no such thing. Their manner grew more and more unfriendly, and their talk among themselves was threatening in tone and expression. Concepción says that those around him demanded that all the Americans be brought over to them, said they wanted our mules, and that our doctor must go with them to care for their wounded. I finally told them that I had no papers, but that Captain Crawford had a letter from the Presidente of Sahuaripa. I sent Concepción over to get this letter from Captain Crawford's coat. He went, and told our folks that I was a prisoner, and that the Mexicans proposed to go with us wherever we went. Our scouts got mad and said that they would take to the mountains before they would go with the Mexicans, whom they could not trust. They jumped up and began to strip for a fight, shaking their guns and calling the Mexicans names. The Mexicans said to me: 'Look at that! They are enemies of ours.' I answered: 'If you detain me here I cannot control my men. You'd better let me go to them.'

"Meantime Concepción had got back with the letter, which they read. It was a very friendly missive from the Presidente of Sahuaripa, recognizing Captain Crawford as an American officer in command of United States troops, telling him where he would probably find the trail of the hostiles, and what depredations they had committed. My captors read this letter over but seemed to think it amounted to nothing. They demanded that I give them six of our government mules for their wounded. I demurred but they insisted, and at last, seeing it the only chance to escape a disastrous fight, I promised them six government mules. Even then they would not let me go until our scouts made that hostile demonstration. Standing up so on the rocks, the strength of our command was then first appreciated by the Mexicans, who were plainly impressed. At last they let me go, having extorted my solemn promise to give them the mules, and sending three or four of their number with me to get the animals. They held Concepción hostage until I sent the mules over and demanded his release.

"My scouts had refrained from firing on the Mexicans, knowing that if they fired, Concepción and I would have been instantly killed. These Indians, taken from a barbarous race and given a trust, kept it faithfully. Fighting for a government whose flag was no protection to them in that alleged friendly country, they showed throughout more honor and forbearance than the Mexicans, who are called civilized. They had endured hunger and fatigue and cold and had taken us through places where no American troops ever went before. They had been marching over those terrific mountains day and night, in rain and cold, and without fires, and at this time, forty-eight hours without food. No men could have been more faithful.

"When I got back to our camp at last and had quieted the scouts, I sent the six mules over to the Mexicans with a note saying that this was all I could do for them, that we wouldn't camp with them as they demanded, and that if they annoyed us further I should call on the Mexican

95

authorities. They sent no receipt for the mules till I sent a note calling for one and further informing them that we were going to leave and that they must not follow us. I then moved out my command under cover, leaving a company of scouts to hold the position until we reached another commanding point, where they rejoined us. When we had gone about three miles, we perceived the Mexicans starting off in the opposite direction, and we saw them no more."

Lieutenant Shipp says: "Captain Crawford lived seven days and four hours after he was shot. We carried him on a litter for two days, eight scouts bearing the litter at a time, all over terribly rough country. It was raining all the time, but we kept him dry. After we met Daly's pack-train from Nacori we fixed one end of the litter to a mule, six scouts carrying the other end. The country was horrible. There was no level ground there, and the utmost we could make was six or seven miles a day. Crawford died on the eighteenth, on the road, about thirty miles from Nacori. On the seventeenth he appeared somewhat conscious, and nodded his head when we came up to him. But he never spoke a word after he was shot. We carried him to Nacori and buried him there with great difficulty. There were only four boards to be found in town for a coffin."

When I showed Crook the dispatch stating that President Diaz, in his message to the Mexican congress, holds that the killing of Crawford was a mistake, the General said earnestly, "The Mexican authorities do all in their power to assist us in running down the renegade Apaches. The Mexicans who attacked Crawford were not regular troops, but simply banditti after scalp-money [government bounty for Indian scalps] and plunder. It was no mistake. They knew who it was. No one ever heard of an Indian or a Mexican making a mistake. American troops might, but Mexicans or Indians never. The only mistake they made was in our numbers. They didn't know how strong our force was, and thought they could get away with it. If they had not attacked Crawford just then, I think this whole Apache business would have been settled then and there. Crawford knew the hostiles and they would have surrendered to him when they wouldn't to any of the others. But they wouldn't have anything to do with the Mexicans, whom they have good reasons for distrusting."

The Diaz message said in part, "The killing of the courageous and deserving officers of both countries is a very lamentable affair, but our troops, which were composed of citizens of the state of Chihuahua, will always have the excuse that they could not take as friends the Indians [of Crawford's command] when they knew well that, according to the agreement for the passing of troops over the frontier, only the regular troops of both republics can pass reciprocally the boundary lines when they are following the hot trail of hostile Indians."

CHAPTER X

FROM TALKS WITH General Crook — who is unapproachable on nothing but his own achievements — and with others who have been able to put a little flesh upon the very bare skeletons he would give me, I have gleaned a very condensed sketch of the old hero's wonderful record. What a nation of ingrates we are! Here is a man who has done more for the frontiers of the United States than any other man living — probably more than any two men. For more than a generation he has been in the active military service of his country, and always successfully. But all this is lost sight of because in this little campaign he has captured only four-fifths of the hostiles! Bah! It makes me

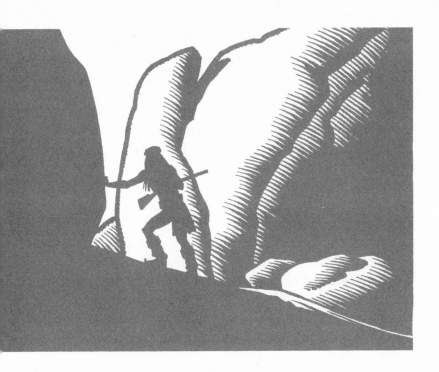

ashamed of my country. Let me refresh your memory a bit as to what this cruelly persecuted man has done.

Born in the Buckeye State, Crook entered West Point July 1, 1848, and graduated four years later with the rank of brevet second lieutenant of the Fourth Cavalry. The following year, a second lieutenant, he entered upon the long series of Indian campaigns in which he has been engaged ever since with the exception of his service in the Civil War. His first work was in northern California and Oregon, and so distinguished were his skill, coolness and courage that the legislature of California voted him a medal before he was first lieutenant.

The Humboldt Indians, then on the war path, engaged his attention, and he made short work of them. The Humboldts had a narrow range and they were "not much force." They were fish eaters, poorly armed and, says the modest general, "they never amounted to anything." His prompt and efficient handling of them, however, laid the foundation of his fame as an Indian fighter.

Having wound up the Humboldts, he was sent to suppress the Rogue Rivers and Shastas, who for years had been harassing the mining regions. These were a hardier race than the Humboldts, inhabited a rougher and more impenetrable country and were better armed. They had the muzzle-loading fire arms of that day, and with sufficient numbers would have proved a very formidable foe. But there were only a few of them and they were soon crushed by the indomitable young lieutenant.

His next service was against the Pitt Rivers, Klamaths and Tollawallas in succession. Here he showed the same brilliant qualities which were already marking him as a coming man, and March 11, 1855, he received a well-earned commission as first lieutenant.

Under Major Garnett in '58, Lieutenant Crook went up to the Yakima country to operate against the federation of Columbia River tribes. These were subjugated in three or four months, Crook winning new laurels in the short campaign.

At the breaking out of the Civil War he entered as captain of the Fourth Infantry, May 14, 1861. Of his honorable career in the war, I need not go into detail. His commissions will show the milestones in his progress. September 17, 1861, he became colonel of the Thirty-sixth Ohio Infantry; September 7 1862, brigadier-general (of volunteers); July 18, 1864, brevet major-general; October

21, 1864, major-general; July 18, 1866, major of the Third Infantry (regular); July 28, 1866, lieutenant-colonel of the Twenty-third Infantry, and he was honorably mustered out January 15, 1866.

From the War of the Rebellion Lieutenant Colonel Crook was called to conquer the Piutes in the far Northwest. He reached Boise City, Idaho, on the eleventh of December, 1866. All through that country the Indians had been a long-standing scourge and terror. "About a week after getting there," said the General with a smile at the recollection, "I took the field with a command of forty men, with my old clothes and a toothbrush, and I didn't see a house again for two years." That army, forty strong, must have seemed very imposing to an officer who had just come from a field where he had commanded an army corps! But if there ever was a man who adapted himself to surroundings it was Crook. He marched out with his handful of men and camped on the trail, sleeping out amid the snow and sagebrush until the last one of the hostiles surrendered, July 4, 1868. It was the first time that the Piutes had been at peace for many a long year. It was a terrible experience, that winter campaign in frozen Idaho. The cold was something awful. There was one time, when the mercury was at its lowest ebb, that the troops broke camp at midnight and marched, half frozen on their saddles, till dawn found them on the edge of the hostile camp. Crook drew up his cavalry and went swooping down on the village. His horse, an old campaigner, took the bit in his teeth, and flashed far ahead of the command and right into the midst of the astounded Indians. It put his brave rider in a decidedly unpleasant predicament. He was between two fires, and the bullets from his own men flew thicker around him than did those of the foe. As soon as possible, Crook dismounted and went to fighting on foot. His troops were now with him, and there was a short fierce struggle among the wickiups. Crook and a red-headed soldier from Boise were making a flank movement together, and in rounding a wickiup, each passed on either side of a small bush. There was a Piute behind that bush; as they reached it "Reddy" got a bullet through his heart. Crook, jumping to one side, perforated the redskin.

Having subjugated the Piutes, a well-armed and warlike race, the strongest against whom Crook had yet been pitted, Crook was sent back after the Pitt Rivers, whom he had conquered eleven years before. His second tussle with them was as successful as the first and taught them a lasting lesson. He not only whipped them, but afterward applied the salve of peaceful teaching.

Thus far the Indians with whom Crook had had to do were tribes of a limited range, mostly in timbered country, and little given to forays of any extent. The Piutes, it is true, were considerable raiders, though nothing compared with the Apaches. Their country was a little like Arizona in some respects, but nothing like as rough. The Apaches had been at their tricks since time immemorial, and there was no doing anything with them. At last, in 1871, the now-celebrated Crook was sent down from the north to try his hand at these indomitable savages. For a year he was so hampered by the corrupt "Indian ring" that he could take no active measures. However he used his time to good advantage drilling a force of Apache scouts, putting in (to use his own words) "the hardest work I ever did." In September 1872 Crook got his hands loose and fell upon the hostile Apaches like a thunderbolt. It was a bloody struggle. The Apaches had not yet learned the art of running away which is now their strongest hold. They stood their ground like men and fought with savage skill. They had not yet acquired the breechloader, either, and in fact most of them were armed only with bows and arrows. Hundreds of them were killed, and still the rest fought on.

It was war upon the heels of war. The Apaches are not a family, but a nation, made up of a host of little tribes — the Chiricahuas, Tontos, Pinals, Arivaipas, Hualapais, Mescaleros, Jicarillas, San Carlos, Warm Springs, Miembres, White Mountains, Coyoteros, Apache Yumas, Apache Mojaves, and so on. The Warm Spring and Miembres Apaches are subdivisions of the Chiricahuas. Campaign followed campaign against tribe after tribe. An intelligent corporal who served under Crook said to me the other day: "In the Tonto campaign in 1872, the General lay out in the rain and snow and sleet for months to get the Tontos when no one else wanted to do it and no one else *would* do it. And after an awful campaign, in which he exposed himself as freely as the commonest soldier, he got them. How he did thrash the Tontos! A lot of them fortified themselves in a cave, and he killed seventy-six of them right there. He pushed them to the wall that way through the whole campaign. I don't believe the Chiricahuas would be on the warpath now if Crook had been let alone. He whipped the other tribes until they were ready to behave. But in 1876, just as he had the Chiricahuas cornered and was about to paralyze them, General O. O. Howard got a special dispensation from the President to treat with them and subdue them by peaceful measures. Howard has said many harsh things of Crook, but the sharpest answer the 'old man' ever allowed himself to make was that, 'in my experience with Indians I have never seen the wisdom of trying to subdue a ferocious tribe by the grace of God.' The logic of events proved that he was right. You have to

hammer those fellows till they are *afraid* to go on the warpath. Crook was never allowed to do this to the Chiricahuas. Howard put them unpunished upon the reservation,
and they soon stampeded into Sonora, carrying out their
usual program of butchery. In '83 they broke out again;
and now [1886 — T. L. F.] they are raiding still. If Crook
had been let at them when he had them within reach, they
would have been as quiet today as the other tribes which
Crook did whip into peace."

Well, Crook made a glorious record. He fought the
Apaches from the Grand Cañon of the Colorado down to
Fort Grant, and from the Little Colorado to the Tucson-
Yuma road. At last, worn out, crushed and humble, the
Apaches came to their Appomattox. At Camp Verde, on
the sixth of April, 1873, they surrendered — five thousand
of them — to the Gray Fox. It broke the backbone of the
Apache nation. Since that time Apache outbreaks have been
merely the sporadic eruptions of a tribe or a small gang of
malcontents. It won a star for the matchless Indian fighter
who had accomplished such results, and on the twenty-
ninth of October 1873 Lieutenant Colonel George Crook
was made Brigadier General Crook. Never was that high
position better earned.

It was with the utmost difficulty that I extracted any information about Crook's activities from himself. He has
little use for newspaper men, and it is only through the
fact that I brought credentials from one of his old comrades in arms [General Harrison Gray Otis — T. L. F.] that
I could approach him on such subjects at all. He is not
starchy in any respect, and talked freely and animatedly
about hunting, fishing and other topics in which we could
meet on common ground. But when it came to what he had

done and to the influences that have fought him in his operations, he closed his lips at once.

The dates and similar outlines of his campaigns he told me, and now and then, warming to some old recollection, some humorous incident in his experience. Speaking of the big surrender above noted reminded him of Delché, then one of the Apache chiefs. Delché was not the George Washington of his tribe. In fact his name means in Apache "the liar." He used to come to the agencies and make peace, picking up a pebble and saying, "When this stone melts, I will change." Then he would turn right around, murder somebody, and be off on the warpath. But when Crook got after him, Delché met his master. At the surrender, he came up to Crook and said: "Last fall I had one hundred and twenty warriors and thought I could lick the world. Now I have only twenty-five. Your copper cartridges have done it. We are all worn out. We are nothing but skin and bones and can't sleep nights. A coyote starts a stone rolling down hill, and we think it is the soldiers coming, and start running. We are tired of running and want to be at peace." Old Shuttlepan, another raiding chief said, "I surrender, not because I love you, but because I fear you — " and the savage scowl on his face emphasized the truth of his words.

"To show their character," said Crook, "take Delché's case. After he was so glad to surrender we put him on the reservation at Verde. After a while he got uneasy and the agent would have been killed right there if it hadn't been for some of our Apache scouts. That night Delché and his whole gang broke out again. They got into the river and rode in it twenty miles, often having to swim their horses. This was to hide their trail. They kept on in the water until they reached a point where a long ledge of rocks runs down into the river, and, riding out on this for some miles without leaving a trail, off they went. About the same time some of the Apaches down here broke out and killed several people. We went after them, chased them down, killed some, and the rest came back. I broke their arrows and smashed their guns. They said they would live quietly on the reservation, but I wouldn't believe them, and I told them that they'd have to go out again and that we'd follow them up and fight them. They begged and begged; and at last I told them that if they would bring me the heads of the seven ringleaders, I would give them another chance. Sure enough they brought me the heads. [I understand from another source that the General was on his porch at headquarters when some of the penitents came up, and, lifting a burlap sack, poured out the seven ghastly trophies before his astonished eyes.] I went up to Verde then and sent for Delché's head. They brought it to me soon. When I got back to San Carlos, somebody else brought me Delché's head! I don't know which was Delché's own head — both looked like him — but it is certain they got all he had, for he never turned up again!"

Crook's work with the Apaches had only its preface in the surrender of April, '73. The conquered tribes were put on reservations throughout the Territory; at last they were consolidated on the White Mountain Reservation. Their conqueror, as great in Indian control as in Indian warfare, bent all his tireless energy and unparalleled experience to making good Indians of them. He taught them with fatherly patience the arts and the value of peace and agriculture. A big man, George Crook. "It is a poor sort of honor," he said to me, "though a popular one, which holds that decency is to be used only toward white folks, and that when you lie to or swindle an Indian, it doesn't count. No one else in the world is so quick to see and to resent any treachery as is the Indian. You can do nothing toward his management unless you have his confidence. True of all men, that is particularly true of him. I have known one of these Apaches to go sixty miles out of his way to ask a man the same question he had asked a month before, and see if he would get the same answer."

"Eventually," said the General, "all their tribal organizations will be broken up. It cannot be done in a moment — it takes time to uproot the institutions of centuries — but it is the inevitable outcome. "Now of course," he will say, "if you have ten thousand troops and one Indian tied down in the middle of them, you don't need any Indian policy. But when you have to *catch* your Indian, there's where the policy begins to be useful. If we could always put our hands on these fellows, the question of managing them would be simple enough. You can bulldoze a lion when you have him in a stout cage and a redhot iron in your hand, but when he is on his native heath the proposition is different. You can't bulldoze these fellows, either, when they are loose in a wilderness as big as Europe."

"Yes," Crook will tell you, "you may fool others as to your intentions, but you can't fool the Indian. He has no books nor newspapers, and so he has to draw on nature for his knowledge. This training has made him wonderfully sharp. He will sit looking at you with the expression of one of those old-fashioned crocks. You've seen them — you can't tell by their looks whether there is honey or vinegar inside. But all this time he is reading you as if you were an open book. He can almost tell from your expression what you had for breakfast!"

It came to be understood throughout the country that

when there was an Indian problem to handle, George Crook was the man to handle it. And so it befell that when in 1875 the Sioux and their allies the Cheyennes and Arapahoes baffled all others, Crook was sent up to Wyoming and Dakota to subdue them. There were fifteen thousand of these Indians — among the most noted savage warriors in the world. They were different from any other Indians with whom Crook had had to do, being a race of centaurs and the most expert horsemen alive, probably. Like other Indians of the plains, they were no good afoot, but mounted on their hardy ponies they were the scourge of their broad range. They had several thousand head of horses, and when a warrior had tired one mount he sprang upon another. During the long winters they were holed up in comfortable quarters. Their ponies got too weak to be of any use for a long time, and they would not start out on a raid until the grass was well up in the spring.

These savage warriors had had everything their own way hitherto. After the famous Fetterman massacre ten years before, they had dictated their own terms. They even made the government evacuate three large forts. Crook settled the Sioux problem. A week after the brave but reckless Custer had thrown away his own life and the lives of his whole command — four companies — by dashing into four thousand to six thousand warriors, Crook, with only a hundred more men than Custer had, met the hostiles, outgeneraled and routed them. He was using the same subtle means of disintegrating them that he had employed down here — using scouts of their own blood against them. I wouldn't rob General Miles of one of his well-earned laurels, but when you talk of Sitting Bull do not forget old Spotted Tail, the real head of the Sioux. Sitting Bull was like Geronimo and some of our newspaper generals of the

Civil War — bigger in type than in the field. Crook sent Spotted Tail away, and made his followers surrender. In 1877, at President Hayes' request, he moved that great body of Indians from a point one hundred miles north of the Northern Pacific down to the Missouri River, a journey of three or four hundred miles, through the rigors of a terrific winter. From that time to 1882 he was in the north, attending to these tribes.

In September, 1881, the famous Juh (pronounced "Hoo"), with Geronimo (then his right-hand man) and both bands, went into Mexico and apparently settled there. Juh lost his life near Casas Grandes, Chihuahua, and thus one of the most dangerous Apaches was removed. He was very drunk one day, and as he rode along a high bluff over the river his mule slipped and they both went down to death. Juh was thirty-six or thirty-seven years old, nearly six feet tall in his moccasins, very dark skinned, and had an impediment in his speech. He was a hard, merciless savage of great determination and a terror all along the border.

American troops were not at that time allowed to cross the line, and the Chiricahuas were safe in Mexico. In the spring of '82, a band of them came up to this country and forced Loco, a chief of the Warm Springs Apaches, to go with them. American troops followed them down below the border, but were met at the northern end of the Sierra Madres by the Mexican General García, who ordered them back. Every Warm Springs and Chiracahua Indian from the reservation was now in Mexico, except Toklonnay, who remained faithful to the Americans from first to last. When Crook came back (September 4, 1882) from his hard work among the Sioux, this was the condition of affairs he found — half a thousand Apaches dwelling in impregnable strongholds far below the Mexican line. They showed no disposition to come north, but Crook with his wonderful knowledge of their character felt certain that it was only a question of time when they would make one of their bloody raids across our border. Foreseeing this, he did everything in his power to avert it. Early in October, 1882, he went down to the Mexican line and tried to open communication with the renegades. Failing in this, he pushed the reorganization of the pack trains of the department, which he had begun immediately upon resuming command, and posted his troops along the frontier at the points whence they could best spring into instant service should the renegades bob up above the line. He also put Captain Crawford and a body of Apache scouts near Cloverdale, New Mexico (once notorious as headquarters for rustlers) to patrol the line from there westward. Some of Crawford's scouts sneaked down below Casas Grandes, Chihuahua, in search of the renegades but could find no trace of them. They had retired into the deeper recesses of the Sierra Madres.

From the time Crook returned to the Department of Arizona to the latter part of March, 1883, there was not a depredation or an outrage of any sort committed in Arizona by any Apache. Crook improved this period of anticipation of a raid from below the border with concientious work among the Indians of the reservation. He impressed upon them the necessity of becoming civilized and self-sustaining; and as an essential to the latter told them that they could select suitable homes anywhere within the reservation, instead of roaming nomadically over it. The head men of the respective bands were to be held responsible for the behavior of their people thus scattered. Some of the brightest, best and most influential of them would be enlisted as soldiers but would reside among the people and assist in leading them toward self-government. Whenever a tribe showed its incapacity for self-control it would be brought into the agency where it could be controlled. If any band became bad, the others must join together and control it. Crook promised to bring in the white soldiers only when the Apaches proved themselves incapable of self-government. One condition of their being allowed to pick out individual homes on the reservation was that they must support themselves after their crops came in in the fall. The chief would be held responsible if any tizwin was made. They must put their spare money into horses and cattle. Their future would depend upon themselves.

At last the event foreseen by Crook came to pass. Early in March, 1883, the renegades became weary of lying idle in the Sierra Madres. A party of about fifty under Geronimo raided into Sonora after stock, while Chatto, one of the most energetic of the Chiricahuas took twenty-five companions to raid into Arizona after a fresh supply of ammunition. Chatto and his band crossed the national line near the Huachuca mountains, March 21, 1883. At sunset the same evening they killed four white men at a charcoal camp twelve miles southwest of Fort Huachuca. One of the raiders was killed in the fight. On the following afternoon they massacred three more men near the Total Wreck mine on the west side of the Whetstone mountains, and the same night crossed the Southern Pacific Railroad near Benson. On the twenty-third, two more men fell victims to the raiders near the south end of the Galiuro mountains.

From there the raiders broke up into small parties, their trails leading across the Pinaleño mountains — the northern extension of the Chiricahua range — across the San Simon valley, and through the Peloncillo mountains to the Gila valley near Ash Springs. All these marches of course were made in the night. The raiders crossed into New Mexico, and on the twenty-eighth, butchered Judge McComas and wife on the stage road between Silver City and Lordsburg and two men on the Gila. As soon as it became known that the renegades had raided from Mexico into Arizona, a general and vigorous pursuit was begun by Crook's forces. But so like lightning was the sweep of the hostiles that pursuit was vain. Their speed is shown by the fact that although they were in Arizona only six days at the outside and in rough country, yet they travelled nearly four hundred miles. Indeed, they had to hurry so that they failed to secure the ammunition which was the object of the raid.

Crook had foreseen, as soon as the news of their presence in the Territory was wired him, that it would in all probability be impossible to catch the raiders by direct pursuit, and while continuing the pursuit with the utmost vigor, he made every possible preparation to intercept their return to Mexico. He immediately telegraphed to the commanding officer at Fort Bowie to scout the Chiricahua mountains and patrol the San Simon and Sulphur Springs valleys, to Fort Thomas to send two companies to Nogales, to Fort Grant to send two companies to White River and to Fort Huachuca to keep the country between the Huachuca and Dragoon mountains thoroughly scouted. To Captain Crawford, Cloverdale, he sent word to put his scouts in position to intercept the raiders if they tried to return through the Stein's Peak range or the Las Animas plains and to Lieutenant Britton Davis at San Carlos to watch closely for them at the reservation. He also by telegraph ordered Lieutenant Gatewood's scouts to Huachuca and all the cavalry at Fort McDowell and four cavalry troops from Fort Apache to

Willcox. All these orders were promptly and conscientiously carried out, the pursuing parties rode their best — and yet not a soul saw one of the raiders! Crook had fenced the boundary line as well as he could, but troops can be put only where there is water — and in this awful land it is a "long time between drinks." As easily as the swallow darts between the poles of a telegraph line the raiders slipped through the necessarily coarse meshes Crook had spread out for them, and sweeping down by night through the mountains on the east side of the Las Animas valley, New Mexico, they reached their strongholds in safety. Crook, who had telegraphed back to Washington for instructions, on the evening of March thirty-first received the following satisfactory reply by telegraph:

"Presidio of San Francisco, March 31, 1883 — *Commanding General Department of Arizona, Sir:* Instructions, just received from the General of the Army, authorize you, under existing orders, to destroy hostile Apaches, to pursue them regardless of department or national lines, and to proceed to such points as you deem advisable. He adds that General Mackenzie's forces will co-operate to the fullest extent.

By order of General Schofield.

(Signed) Kelton, A.A.G."

Crook immediately hurried by rail to Guaymas and Hermosillo in Sonora and to the city of Chihuahua in the state of the same name to consult with the Mexican authorities, civil and military, as to an amicable arrangement for "carrying the war into Africa." He says: "The reception extended to me was of the most hospitable and cordial character. Generals Carbo and Topete and their staffs in Sonora, and General Torres and other prominent functionaries in that State; Governors Samaniego and Terrazas, of the State of Chihuahua; Mayor Zubiran, of the city of Chihuahua, and other gentlemen — all gave assurance that they would in every possible way aid in the subjection of the Chiricahuas who had for so many years murdered and plundered the Mexican people as well as our own. Consuls Willard, at Guaymas, and Scott, at Chihuahua, rendered me valuable assistance."

These important details arranged, Crook started for San Bernardino Springs on the Mexican line, arriving there April twenty-ninth with his forces. Before burying himself in the Sierra Madres it was necessary to protect the rear and flanks of his expedition and to protect the settlers of Arizona from raids during his absence. For this double purpose Crook made the following disposition of troops: Major James Biddle was left with five companies of the Third and Sixth Cavalry at Silver Creek; Captain G. E. Overton with two companies of Sixth Cavalry at old Camp Rucker; Captain P. D. Vroom with two companies of Third Cavalry at Calabasas. These troops, in conjunction with those from Fort Bowie under Captain Rafferty, and from Fort Huachuca under Major Nolan, were to patrol the country with all possible thoroughness. Colonel E. A. Carr, Sixth Cavalry, was authorized to assume general command of these forces should it at any time become necessary. Captain Wm. E. Dougherty, commanding officer at Fort Apache, was sent back to his post to attend to the control of the Apaches on the reservation.

Everything being prepared, Crook now opened the campaign, May first, leaving San Bernardino Springs with the following force: a hundred and ninety-three Apache scouts under Captain Emmet Crawford, Third Cavalry, Lieutenant C. B. Gatewood, Sixth Cavalry, and Lieutenant J. O.

Mackey, Third Cavalry; forty-two enlisted men of the Sixth Cavalry under Captain A. R. Chaffee and Lieutenants Frank West and W. W. Forsyth. Acting Assistant Surgeon George Andrews and Hospital Steward J. B. Sweeney accompanied the expedition. Crook's personal staff consisted of Captain John G. Bourke and Lieutenant Fiebiger. "This," says Crook, " was the maximum force which could be supplied by the use of every available pack-animal in the department (over three hundred and fifty animals in excellent condition); and the minimum with which I could hope to be successful in the undertaking upon which I had engaged. We had supplies, field rations for sixty days, and one hundred and fifty rounds of ammunition to the man. To reduce baggage, officers and men carried only such clothing and bedding as was absolutely necessary, and instead of keeping up their own messes, the officers shared the food of the packers."

On the twenty-seventh of March, while the hostiles were raiding up here, one of their number had deserted them, and was arrested by Lieutenant Davis and turned over to Crook. Pe-nal-tishn, commonly nicknamed "Peaches," after a severe cross-examination, had agreed to lead Crook to the hostile stronghold; under the guidance of this Chiricahua the expedition started out into the savage and unknown fastness of the Sierra Madres.

Crossing the line into Mexico, the expedition followed down the San Bernardino River, the northernmost branch of the Yaqui. For three days they did not encounter a soul. The whole region through which they were passing had been depopulated by the Apaches, and great areas of former farms had become a jungly waste of mesquite and canebrake. They followed the hostile trail deeper and deeper into the wilderness, conducted by Peaches. On the sixth of May the expedition passed the Sonoran hamlets of Bavispe, San Miguel and Basaraca, whose inhabitants were wild with joy. They had good cause to welcome the coming of Crook. Their condition was deplorable. In all these little villages the swoop of the Apache was to be looked for at any moment. The people were absolutely cowed, and no man dared venture a couple of miles from home. It was such a reign of terror as obtains among the hamlets of India when the maneater prowls in the neighboring jungle. The people of Bavispe offered Crook the assistance of all their able-bodied men, but he declined for want of transportation and supplies. He also declined their proffer of four guides to the Sierra Madres, knowing that the Apache trailers he already had were matchless.

Moving cautiously and by night to escape detection, Crook's force entered the Sierra Madres on the eighth of May. It was evident that they were approaching the stronghold of the hostiles. Indian sign became abundant, and the invaders came upon abandoned camps which had been occupied by fifteen, twenty, thirty and even forty families; and upon cattle, horses and burros, alive and dead. The country was indescribably rugged — lofty and inaccessible mountains, dizzy cañons and frowning cliffs — as Crook's description shows. "I remember one night we camped in a deep cañon," said the general. "The next morning at daybreak we began to climb the sides, zig-zagging to the top. Then after travelling about half a mile on top of the ridge, down we had to go into another cañon. *We were all day in going six miles!*"

I remarked that one of the most striking proofs of the roughness of the country was the accidents among mules, for a good many of these sure-footed animals were killed or crippled by tumbling down the terrific precipices. Gen-

116

eral Crook replied that pack animals seldom fall unless they are pushed. "The old ones, particularly, know mighty well where they can go and where they can't, and when they come to a dangerous place they will stop and you can't budge them with a club. But the others, coming up behind, will frequently crowd them off, and down they go. I remember once one of our mules fell twenty-five hundred feet. The trail ran along a narrow shelf at the top of a tremendous precipice, and this old fellow got shoved off by his mates. The doctor was down in the valley below and saw that whole thing. He says that when the mule came over the edge, it didn't look any bigger than a jackrabbit. When it struck on the rocks at the bottom, it exploded like a bomb, and he couldn't find a piece as big as his hand. The animal had all our cooking outfit on his back, too, and we were left in a bad plight. On another occasion a mule in the pack train with which I was messing got pushed off the trail on the side of an extremely steep mountain. Loaded with bacon, he went rolling down until he disappeared from our sight in a cloud of dust. There were two packers way down the zig-zag trail, and they declare that the mule bounced clear over them, struck on his back on a big rock below, bounced way up into the air, and finally went souse into a deep pool in the river, whence he swam out and went to grazing on the grass beyond!"

In such a region travel was of course arduous and slow. It was necessary also to use the utmost caution in proceeding, to guard against ambushes and against alarming the wary foe. There were advantages, however, not usually found in Apache-hunting — an abundance of pure water and good fuel, the mountains being covered with oak and pine and full of running streams.

On the twelfth of May, Peaches led the command to the

enemy's stronghold, a fortified point far up among the rocks and absolutely impregnable to attack. "For that matter," says Crook — and so say all who have been in that section — "The whole Sierra Madre is a natural fortress, and to drive the Chiricahuas from it by any other methods than those we employed would have cost hundreds of lives." Reaching the stronghold they found that the enemy, Apache-like, had already evacuated. Bred to a warfare which is made up of surprises, the Apache never stays in the same camp more than a few days at the outside. By continual shifting he avoids much of the probability of being caught unawares. He never goes into camp, even for a night, without securely fortifying himself, but no place can be sufficiently fortified to satisfy him as a permanent fortress.

But though the hostiles had moved on, it was evident that they were not far away. So Crook left the pack trains in the stronghold under guard of Captain Chaffee's company and sent out Crawford and the Apache scouts to scour the country thoroughly in front and on both flanks.

On the fifteenth of May, the scouts struck the hostile camps, which proved to be occupied by the forces of Chatto and Bonito. Crook had given careful directions for surrounding these camps, but some of the scouts imprudently fired on a buck and a squaw whom they espied and a general fight ensued, lasting several hours. The hostiles were completely routed, nine or more being killed, while five half-grown boys and girls were captured along with all the contents of the camps. Among the captured stuff was much that had been stolen by the raiders from Mexicans and Americans, including forty horses and mules.

The hostiles were now so thoroughly alarmed that to pursue them was out of the question. They had scattered among the countless rugged peaks, whose every rock was a fortress from behind which the Indians could deal back death with their breech-loading rifles. There were but two alternatives. One was to go back to the United States, wait until the Chiricahuas felt secure and then attempt to surprise them again. The other was to get them to surrender. The eldest of the girls captured in Chatto's camp said that if they would let her go she would call in some of her people for a pow-wow. She appeared sincere, and Crook allowed her to go. Next day the scouts made a signal smoke, and six squaws came in. Crook refused to parley with them, telling them that he would talk business only with representative men of their tribe. These they went out to fetch. Early on the morning of May eighteenth, Chihuahua came in and had a long talk with Crook. He said they had supposed the Sierra Madres to be impregnable — none of their enemies had ever penetrated their fastnesses before. The Mexican troops never got beyond the foothills. The Chiricahuas didn't waste bullets on their besiegers but simply rolled rocks down on them. Chihuahua expressed the universal Apache hatred for the Mexicans, saying that the Mexicans took care to kill the Chiricahua woman and children, but ran away from the men and treated them all with treachery. Shortly before this the Mexicans had invited a group of Chiricahuas into a small town near Casas Grandes with every show of hospitality, had got them drunk and then murdered a number, making prisoners of the rest. Chihuahua said the Chiricahuas would be glad to settle down in peace. They were tired of this incessant warring.

After Chihuahua, the rest of the Chiricahuas came flocking from all directions. Among them were the chiefs Geronimo, Chatto, Bonito, Loco, Nachita and Keowtennay. The latter had never been on the reservation, having been born and reared in the Sierra Madres. All surrendered. This brought into Crook's hands over five hundred hostiles, including a hundred and twenty bucks. They wanted to make peace and go back on the reservation, but Crook told them no, he was tired of their disobedience and outbreaks. The best thing they could do was to stay right there and he would stay and fight it out with them. He kept them on this ragged edge for several days, and each day they became more worried and more importunate, till at last they fairly begged him to take them back to San Carlos. Geronimo and the others said, "We give ourselves up. Do with us as you please."

This is what Crook wanted. He took them at their word. It is worthy of remembering that Crook did not disarm any of the renegades, but took them as they were. Rations were now running short and with this great number of prisoners on his hands it was all Crook could do to get back to the base of supplies without starving. He started homeward at once therefore, the Chiricahuas sending out runners to call in their stragglers who were scattered all over that frightfully broken country. Crook marched north, accompanied by such of the prisoners as had come in, while all the rest came straggling along behind as they received the news. Although Crook had only about two hundred and forty men and the renegades numbered some five hundred, fully armed, *every one came to the reservation.*

Crook's habit of not demanding the arms of any of his prisoners at their surrender has been damned so widely by those who know nothing of the subject upon which they are so fond of exploiting their ignorance, that I append the excellent reasons he gives in his official report:

"It is not advisable to let an Indian think you are afraid of him even when fully armed. Show him that at his best he is no match for you. It is not practicable to disarm Indians. Their arms can never be taken from them unless they are captured while fighting with their arms in their hands, by sudden surprise, or disabling wounds. When Indians first surrender or come upon a reservation, they anticipate being disarmed, and make their preparations in advance. They cache most of their best weapons and deliver up only the surplus and unserviceable. The disarming of Indians has in almost every instance on record proved a farcical failure. Let me cite the case of the Cheyennes who surrendered in 1878. They were searched with the greatest care when they were confined, and, it was believed, with the fullest success. Yet when they broke out of prison at Fort Robinson, Nebraska, they were all well armed with guns and knives and ammunition. Doubtless their weapons had been taken apart and the pieces concealed by the women under their clothing, for weeks prior to the outbreak. It is unfair, furthermore, to deprive the Indian of the means of protecting his home and his property against the white scoundrels who, armed to the teeth, infest the border, and would consider nothing so worthy of their prowess as the plunder of ponies or other property from unarmed Indians just beginning to plant crops or raise stock. So long as the white thieves roam the country, so long should the Indians at San Carlos be allowed to carry arms for their own protection."

This further instance of Crook's assumption that the Apache is after all a human being is one of the reasons why Arizona is down on him — that is, the bloviating element of Arizona; it is a significant fact that the old Arizonans who have been here from ten to twenty years believe in Crook. It is the later rabble that hounds him. But his belief in Apache humanity (not humaneness) is bound to win. Crook has no silly sentimentalism, no maudlin mercy; but he knows what can and what cannot be done.

"In dealing with this question," Crook says, "I could not lose sight of the fact that the Apache represents generations of warfare and bloodshed. From his earliest infancy he has had to defend himself against enemies as cruel as the beasts of the mountains and forests. In his brief moments of peace, he constantly looks for attack or ambuscade, and in his almost constant warfare no act of bloodshed is too cruel or unnatural. It is, therefore, unjust to punish him for violations of a code of war which he has never learned, and which he cannot understand. He has, in almost all of his combats with white men, found that his women and children were the first to suffer; that neither age nor sex is spared. In surprise attacks on camps women and children are killed in spite of every precaution; this cannot be prevented by any foresight or orders of the commander any more than shells fired into a beleaguered city can be prevented from killing innocent citizens or destroying private property. Nor does this surprise the Apache, since it is in accordance with his own mode of fighting. With this fact before us we can understand why he should be ignorant of the rules of civilized warfare. All that we can reasonably do is to keep him under such supervision that he cannot plan new outbreaks without running the risk of immediate detection; for these *new* acts of rascality, punish him so severely that he will know we mean no nonsense. As rapidly as possible, make a distinction

123

between those who mean well and those who secretly desire to remain as they are. Encourage the former and punish the latter. Let the Apache see that he has something to gain by proper behavior and something to lose by not falling in with the new order of things. Sweeping vengeance is as much to be deprecated as silly sentimentalism. . . .

"The Chiricahuas of today are no worse than were the rest of the Apaches, six thousand in number, who were driven upon the reservation in 1873. The task of managing that number was more formidable than that of looking after the Chiricahuas can ever be; but it was accomplished without any trouble, except such as was stirred up by greedy white men. Many of the Apache chiefs of that day were sullenly opposed to the new order of things. They were ferreted out and broken of their power for mischief, while those who favored the ways of civilization were supported by every influence we could bring to bear."

Well, Crook and his five hundred captives got back safely. The campaign had lasted from May first to June ninth, and was in every respect a success. The prisoners were put upon the reservation and the influence of civilization were brought to bear upon them. For two years there was not an outrage or a depredation of any kind committed by the Apache. The civilizing powers had much to contend against; and at last — incited by a thousand little causes — there came the outbreak of a year ago.

I have had the good fortune to secure a copy of General Crook's final report from the Department of Arizona. It has come to me entirely without knowledge on the General's part. It is so full of interest that I will let Crook tell of his last campaign against the Apaches with his own pen.

"HEADQUARTERS, DEP'T OF ARIZONA,
IN THE FIELD, FORT BOWIE, A. T.

April 10, 1886

Adjutant General, Division of the Pacific,
Presidio of San Francisco, California.

SIR: — I have the honor to submit the following report of the operations of the troops under my command in the pursuit of hostile Chiricahuas.

My first information of impending trouble was a telegram received on the afternoon of May 17, 1885; and before a reply could be sent, the wires between Fort Apache and San Carlos were cut. The next afternoon I was informed that Geronimo, Nanay, Mangus, Natchez, and Chihuahua, with a considerable party, had left their camp just after dark the preceding evening. Within a few days the exact number of renegades was fixed at thirty-four men, eight well grown boys and ninety-two women and children. I learned that on May fifteenth Lieutenant Britton Davis, Third Cavalry, sent a telegraphic dispatch to me, which I did not see until months afterwards. Had this telegram reached me, I feel morally certain that the troubles would have been settled without an outbreak. Troubles of minor importance were consequently occurring on the Reservation, which were quieted down by the officers in charge reporting them to me and receiving my instructions. There would probably not have been as much danger or difficulty in managing the matter reported by Lieut. Davis's telegram as there was in quelling the disturbances started by Ka-e-te-na in March and June, 1884, in which Bonito was implicated, or those in July, 1885. I have not on hand papers relating to the management of those difficulties; but in each instance methods were employed suitable to the special emergency. This trouble arose from a

125

tizwin drunk; and in order to shield the guilty parties, all the prominent chiefs drank of this liquor, and in a body went to Lieut. Davis and informed him of the fact, thinking that in this way all would escape punishment. Lieut. Davis told them that in a matter of such importance he could not take action himself, but would report the whole occurrence to me for my directions. Lieut. Davis wrote the telegram in the presence of the Indians, told them what he had written, and said that he should act in accordance with my personal instructions, and would notify them what my orders were when received. A messenger was immediately sent with this dispatch to Fort Apache, but no reply was received. The Indians waited until dark, and again assembled the next day, but receiving no reply became alarmed, and doubtless concluded that I was making preparations to seize the whole of them and punish them as I had Ka-e-te-na. This idea, I afterward learned, had been put in their heads by ill-disposed persons on the Reservation. A matter of this kind, while it must be managed with exceeding caution, must be settled promptly — without giving time for their suspicious imaginations to work upon their fears. Delay is a fatal error. . . .

Within an hour after the renegades left their camp on Turkey Creek, two troops of the Fourth Cavalry, under command of Capt. Allen Smith, and a party of White Mountain and Chiricahua scouts, under Lieuts. Gatewood and Davis, left Fort Apache in pursuit. But such was the rapidity of their flight that it was impossible to overtake them. It subsequently transpired that they had traveled nearly 120 miles before stopping for rest or food.

As soon as the departure of the Indians was known, troops were immediately put in motion to endeavor to overtake or intercept them. . . . and every effort was made to warn citizens, at all points within reach, of their danger.

On the 28th of May, my information indicating that the Indians had gone into the Black Range, New Mexico, I left my headquarters and proceeded to Fort Bayard, whence I could more intelligently direct the movement of troops from my department. The whole country, north, east and west of Bayard was filled with troops. No less than 20 troops of cavalry and more than 100 Indian scouts were moved in every direction, to either intercept or follow the trail of the hostiles. But with the exception of the capture of a few of their animals by the Indian scouts under Chatto, and a slight skirmish with their rear guard by the troops from Apache under Capt. Smith on May 22, in which three of his command were wounded — the hostiles were not even caught sight of by the troops, and finally crossed in to Mexico about June 10th.

In the twenty-three days from the outbreak until the Indians crossed into Mexico, every possible effort was made by the troops, which were pushed to the limit of endurance of men and animals, but without result other than to drive the Indians out of the Black Range and Mogollons, and also to save the lives, probably, of many ranchmen and prospectors. It must be remembered that the two years of peace had enormously increased the business interests of Arizona and the contiguous portions of New Mexico. Cattle and horse ranches had been established wherever a mountain stream afforded the necessary water. Thus the hostiles found food and transportation in every valley; whereas the pursuing troops were limited to the horses they were riding and to the rations carried on their pack-trains. The vigor of the pursuit may be understood from the fact that more than 150 horses and mules were found on the different trails — worn out and killed, or abandoned by the Indians in their flight.

As soon as it became evident that the Indians were moving south, I proceeded to Deming, June 5, and began preparations to follow them into Mexico.

Captain Emmet Crawford, Third Cavalry who had reported to me, was ordered with the battalion of scouts which had been operating in the country about the old Warm Spring Reservation, to go to Separ by rail, and thence move with a troop of cavalry to the south end of the Animas Valley, with the hope that the hostiles might cross into Mexico through the Guadalupe Mountains. The result showed that the main body of the hostiles crossed the Line on the west of the Mule Mountains, though a small party surprised a camp of the 4th Cav. in Guadalupe Cañon, guarded by seven enlisted men, of whom they killed four. Another small party crossed the Line near Lake Palomas. Lieut. Davis — who, with sixty White Mountain and Chiricahua scouts, had been following the trail of the hostiles as rapidly as possible — was ordered to report to Capt. Crawford. On the 11th of June the combined force. . . followed the hostiles into the Sierra Madre. On the 9th of June a telegram was received from Lieutenant-General Sheridan, informing me that I was authorized to enlist 200 additional scouts; and that the Cheyenne pack-train had been ordered to report to me. I was also directed to establish my headquarters at a point either on or near the S. P. R. R. I accordingly proceeded to Fort Bowie. Directions were immediately issued for the enlistment of the new scouts — 100 at San Carlos, and the remainder at Fort Apache. As soon as the 100 at Apache were enlisted, Lieut. Gatewood was ordered in command, to thoroughly scout the Mogollons and the Black Range, in order to determine definitely whether any of the hostiles were remaining in that region, as was persistently reported. This movement delayed his arrival at Bowie about twenty days; and though it was found, as I had expected, that there were no hostiles in New Mexico, I did not deem it advisable to organize a second expedition for service in Mexico until this fact was definitely established.

As soon as necessary preparations could be completed, Capt. Wirt Davis, Fourth Cavalry, with a command consisting of his own cavalry troops and 100 Indian scouts, with pack-trains carrying sixty days' rations, was ordered into Mexico. My plan of operations was as follows: that the commands of Capts. Davis and Crawford should thoroughly scour the Sierra Madre and the adjoining mountain ranges, and endeavor to surprise the hostile camps in Mexico; at the same time I would so station troops along the border as to prevent, if possible, the return of the renegades to the United States when they should be driven out of Mexico by the commands operating in the mountains. With this in view, I placed a troop of cavalry at every water hole along the border from the Patagonia mountains to the Rio Grande. With each troop I stationed a detachment of Indian scouts, with sufficient pack mules to carry at least ten days' rations for the command. Orders were given to conceal the troops, and to keep the country between the different camps constantly patrolled. I also established a second line nearer the railroad, as reserves to the first line. In order to insure prompt supplies to the commands operating in Mexico, I established a depot at Lang's ranch, at the south end of the Animas Valley, near the boundary. In New Mexico reserve camps were also established at such points as seemed to offer the best facilities for rapid movement and successful pursuit, in the event that the renegades should return to the United States. Four troops of the Eighth Cavalry, from Texas, having reported to Gen. Bradley, were stationed north of the railroad, at points which were deemed most available for pursuit of the Indians, and most likely to afford protection to life and property.

On the 23rd of June, Capt. Crawford's scouts under Chatto struck Chihuahua's band in the Bavispe mountains, northeast of Oputo; but owing to the position occupied by the hostiles, their camp could not be surrounded, and in the fight which ensued, they escaped. Fifteen women and children, a number of horses and a considerable amount of plunder were captured.

Capt. Davis crossed into Mexico, July 13, and after much severe fatigue succeeded in locating the camp of a band of hostiles under Geronimo in the Sierra Madre, a little north-east of Nacori. The camp was attacked by a picked detail of seventy-three scouts, under Lieut. Day, Ninth Cavalry, and, though the surprise was complete, it is now believed that the only hostiles killed were one squaw and two boys. Everything in the camp was captured, with fifteen women and children. . . .

Captains Davis and Crawford continued scouting in the mountains, and their commands endured uncomplainingly almost incredible hardships and fatigues. But the hostiles were so continually on the alert that no other engagement was had until, on September 22d, Capt. Davis again struck a band of about 20 hostiles in the Terez Mountains. In the fight that ensued, one of the scouts was killed. The hostiles, having been driven out of Mexico by the scouts, crossed into the United States through Guadalupe cañon, within a few miles of a camp of two troops of cavalry, about daylight on the morning of Sept. 28th. They were closely followed by both Captains Davis and Crawford. It being evident that the hostiles intended to raid the White Mountain Reservation, or go into the Mogollons or Black Range, New Mexico, dispositions were made to prevent this. Cavalry was directed from different points by converging routes toward the Gila. Troops were established in positions to prevent the hostiles crossing the San Simon valley into the Stein's Peak range; and others were placed along the railroad where they could be available for instant transportation by rail to threatened points. The scouts followed the hostiles, and several troops of cavalry were moved to points where it was thought possible to ambush them. The renegades took the roughest possible trails over the Chiricahua Mountains, and twice endeavored to cross the San Simon valley, but each time were frightened back into the Chiricahuas by seeing the dust of moving columns, or discovering their trails across the valley. They then crossed the Sulphur Springs valley by night into the Dragoons, whither they were followed by Crawford's scouts. They fled through this range, back into the valley, and south toward the Mule mountains. Here their trail suddenly turned sharp to the east and went back into the Chiricahuas, Crawford and his scouts following persistently. The stock of the hostiles was by this time worn out; and though they had gathered all that was possible along the route, they were finally absolutely dismounted, and the troops were in such position that it seemed probable that the entire band would be captured or killed. But at this juncture they succeeded in remounting themselves with the best stock in the country; and finding that it would be impossible to get north of the railroad, they returned to Mexico. Capt. Viele, Tenth Cavalry, followed them, with two troops, as far as Ascencion, Chihuahua; from which point, further pursuit being useless, he returned with his jaded command to his camp in Cave Cañon.

The remounting of the hostiles was in this instance particularly exasperating. The cattlemen of the San Simon had gathered in White Tail Cañon, on the east side of the Chiricahuas, for the beginning of their fall round-up. In spite of the warnings which they received the evening before, that hostiles on foot had been seen in the vicinity, they lariated their cow ponies, the best stock in the country, around a ranch in which they all slept. In the morning all their stock except two or three were gone, and the hostiles had secured about thirty of the finest horses in Arizona. This is not an isolated instance. Several times before and since parties of hostiles have been dismounted by persistent pursuit, and escaped in the same way by securing remounts — and this, too, in spite of constant warning and importunities to ranchmen to secure their stock. The Indians acted as if they could take stock with perfect impunity. At one time they took a quantity of horses from a corral belonging to the Sulphur Springs Cattle Company under circumstances that make it evident that several men who were in the ranch-house knew what was going on. Although there were only three Indians in the raiding party, no attempt was made to prevent the stock from being taken. At another time, early in June, a party of Indians, numbering perhaps a dozen men and 40 or 50 squaws and children, drove up and shot several beeves within a mile of the largest ranch in Arizona, in broad daylight. There were 20 cowboys on the ranch at the time, all fully armed, and yet the Indians went into camp, cooked the meat, and finally left, sometime during the night. During all this time, not the slightest attempt was made to interfere with them, or even to give information to the troops.

The hostiles having returned to Mexico the troops were sent back to their field stations. The scouts having been constantly on the march since the beginning of operations, and the terms of service of many of them having expired, it was thought best to discharge them and enlist others; and, while the new commands were being organized, to refit and reorganize, as thoroughly as possible, the pack-trains, which were by this time almost worn out. The new commands were fitted out as soon as possible; and, on November 27th, Captain Davis again started into Mexico. Captain Crawford was detained by a fruitless pursuit of a raiding party under Ulzanna, and did not cross the line until about two weeks later.

The raid of the party of 11 hostiles who succeeded in eluding the troops on the line and went up into New Mexico by the Lake Palomas trail early in November . . . is mentioned as showing the dangers and difficulties to be contended against from small parties. During the period of about four weeks this band traveled probably not less than 1200 miles, killed 38 people, captured and wore out 250 head of horses; and, though twice dismounted, succeeded in crossing back into Mexico, with the loss of but one man, who was killed by loyal Indians, whose camp they attacked near Fort Apache. At one time it seemed probable that the band would be captured, but the refusal of a party of forty Navajo scouts, under Lieut. Scott, Thirteenth Infantry, to follow the trail, although supported by a troop of cavalry, caused the pursuit to be abandoned, owing to the inability of the troops to follow the trail of the hostiles in the mountains, and a severe storm of snow and rain coming on, which lasted three days and obliterated all trails as fast as made, so that the raiders were enabled to choose their own route into Mexico.

For details connected with the movements of Capt. Davis's command in Mexico, I respectfully refer to the attached reports of this officer . . . . The first expedition of Capt. Crawford is well covered by the report of Lieut. Britton Davis. . . . It is to be regretted that the death of Capt. Crawford — at a time when there is reason to believe that, had he lived, he would have received the unconditional surrender of Geronimo, Natchez, and their bands — has prevented a detailed report of all the operations pertaining to his first expedition. . . .

It appears that on the 10th of January, Capt. Crawford — after an exceedingly difficult night march — attacked the hostile camp, near the Haros river, about sixty miles below Nacori. Though the attack did not result in the destruction of the hostiles, for the reasons shown, yet the scouts captured all the hostiles' stock and supplies of every description, and convinced them that they could never find a secure resting place. The hostiles accordingly asked for a conference with Capt. Crawford, to take place the next morning. What the results of that conference would have been cannot, of course, be positively stated; but he was thoroughly known to all the Indians, and had their confidence; and it is believed that he was the only white man besides myself who could have induced the hostiles to surrender. Unfortunately the scouts — worn out by three days' incessant marching, for forty-eight hours without food; and, under the circumstances, fearing no attack by the hostiles, did not keep watch that night with their usual vigilance. The morning of the 11th, before full daylight, they were attacked in their sleep by 154 Mexicans. By the first volley three of the scouts were wounded before they could get the shelter of the rocks. By the exertions of their officers the firing was stopped, and every effort was made to explain to the Mexicans that they were attacking a friendly force. The Mexicans were told in Spanish that the Indians were American scouts, and that the officers in command were American officers. During this interval the Mexicans approached so near that their words could be distinguished. Capt. Crawford took his position on a rock, without arms, within easy speaking distance of them. He pointed out that he was in uniform. At the same time Mr. Horn, the interpreter, was explaining who they were. Suddenly, without warning, a Mexican, within about twenty or thirty yards of Capt. Crawford, raised his piece and fired. Crawford, fell, shot through the brain. This shot seemed to be the agreed-upon signal, as at once the firing became general. Mr. Horn was shot through the arm; but though the firing lasted several minutes [over half an hour] and was only stopped after the Mexicans had lost their commanding officer and the second in command, with at least two others killed and several wounded, not one of the scouts was touched. Had it not been for the exertions of Lieuts. Maus and Shipp and the two Chiefs-of-Scouts, who finally succeeded in stopping the firing of the scouts, many more of the attacking party would have been killed.

In the light of the events of the day following — when Lieut. Maus was detained by force in the Mexican camp, and was only allowed to return [to his own camp] when his scouts began to strip for action, and upon his word of honor that he would send them [the Mexicans] six of his eleven pack mules — the conclusion reached by Lieut. Maus, that the Mexicans knew whom they were attacking, is almost (in) controvertible. *The death of Capt. Crawford was, in any event, an assassination. . . .*

The day following the Mexican attack, the hostiles again asked to talk; but Crawford was insensible, practically dead, (though his death did not actually occur until the eighth day), and the interview of the hostiles with Lieut. Maus resulted in their expressing a wish for a conference with myself at a point indicated — about twenty-five miles south of San Bernadino. This conference took place in the Cañon de Los Embudos on the 25th of March. I found the hostiles encamped on a rocky hill, surrounded by ravines and cañons through which they could escape to the higher peaks behind, in the event of an attack. They were in superb physical condition, armed to the teeth, and supplied with all the ammunition they could carry. In manner they were suspicious, and at the same time confident and self-reliant. Lieut. Maus, with his battalion of scouts, was camped on lower ground, separated by a deep rugged cañon from their position, and distant five or six hundred yards. The hostiles refused to allow any nearer approach.

I was conscious that in agreeing to meet them I was placing myself in a position similar to that in which Gen. Canby lost his life, and that any incident which might — with or without cause — excite their suspicions, would result in my death and probably that of some of the officers with me. I therefore endeavored to induce the hostiles to meet me within the United States, urging that the presence of white soldiers would prevent any attempt of the Mexicans to attack them. But no argument would move them. . . .

That night I got emissaries into their camp, but the hostiles were so excited that they would listen to nothing. The friendly Indians whom I employed as emissaries told me that they dared not even talk to the hostiles of surrendering. Geronimo told his people to keep their guns in their hands, and to be ready to shoot at a moment's notice. The friendly Indians said that the slightest circumstance which might look suspicious would be a signal for firing to begin; that the hostiles would kill all they could, and scatter in the mountains. Even after they surrendered to me they did not relax their vigilance. They kept mounted and constantly on the watch; there were never more than five to eight of their men in our camp at one time; and even after the march northward began, the hostiles did not keep together, but scattered over the country in parties of two or three. At night they camped in the same way; and, had I desired it, it would have been absolutely impossible to seize more than half a dozen of them. The remainder would have escaped, and our breach of faith would have prevented forever any possibility of any settlement with them.

The last conference with the hostiles took place on the afternoon of March 27th. That night whisky or mescal was smuggled into their camp, and many of them were drunk. The next morning Chihuahua reported this fact, but told me they would all begin to move [north — T. L. F.] toward the border. In order to be in telegraphic communication with the War Department, I deemed it essential to return to Fort Bowie immediately, and I accordingly left the camp, leaving there my interpreters and the trusted Indians whom I had employed in the negotiations, with Lieut. Maus — who, with his battalion of scouts, was to conduct the hostiles to Fort Bowie. The first day the command marched to the supply camp, about twelve miles south of San Bernardino; and next day they camped at Smuggler's Springs, near the Border. Owing to the persistent sale of intoxicating liquor to the hostiles by a man named Tribolet, I gave directions that his ranch should be so guarded that no liquor

137

could be had by the Indians. It seems that from the time the scouts had been in camp, south of San Bernardino, this man had been selling them large quantities of liquor; and that when the hostiles came in, he began selling to them — and boasted of the large amount of money he was making on the traffic. The exertions of Lieut. Maus and his officers did not prevent the hostiles from obtaining liquor from this same source on the night of the 29th, although the day before all the liquor which could be discovered by careful search (some fifteen gallons) had been destroyed.

The night of the 29th the hostiles were apparently sober; and two dispatches from Lieut. Maus to me indicated that there would be no difficulty in continuing the march without trouble. But the Indians were in such a condition of mind that any remark with reference to what would happen to them when they finally got into my power excited them. It is understood, and I believe, that such remarks were made by interested parties; and in consequence thereof, Geronimo and Natchez, with twenty bucks, stampeded during the night, taking with them two horses and one mule, fourteen women and two young boys. Several days afterward two of the bucks returned. They said they were sleeping together, and heard their people leaving camp, whereupon — supposing something to be wrong — they left also. Next morning they concluded that there was no reason why they should leave, and they started back, voluntarily rejoining Lieut. Maus about fifteen miles from this post.

After the most careful inquiry, I am satisfied that no one in the camp, except those who left, knew anything about it until next morning; and it is probable that a number of those who left were frightened out at the last moment. Under the circumstances, it would have been impossible to prevent their escaping. Lieut. Maus, with 80 scouts of his battalion, immediately started in pursuit. Capt. Dorst, Fourth Cavalry, was also put upon the trail.

The remainder of the prisoners arrived at Fort Bowie on April 2d, and on the 7th, in compliance with telegraphic instructions from the Secretary of War, left Bowie Station by train, under charge of First Lieut. J. R. Richards, Jr., Fourth Cavalry, under escort of a company of the Eighth Infantry, for Fort Marion, St. Augustine, Florida. They numbered seventy-seven — fifteen bucks, thirty-three women, and twenty-nine children. . . . By this surrender the entering wedge has been driven; and it is believed that there will be but little difficulty in obtaining the surrender of those who are still out. . . .

Before closing this report I desire to express my appreciation of the conduct of the officers and men of my command during the dreary months they have been engaged in this discouraging and well-nigh hopeless task. Where all have done well, it seems invidious to mention names of individuals. All . . . bore uncomplainingly the almost incredible fatigues and privations, as well as the dangers, incident to these operations.

> Very respectfully,
> Your obedient servant,
> GEORGE CROOK,
> *Brigadier General Commanding.*"

CHAPTER **XI**

GENERAL MILES is a tall, straight, fine-looking man, of two hundred ten pounds weight, and apparently in the early fifties. He has a well-modeled head, high brow, strong eye, clean-cut aquiline nose and firm mouth — an imposing and soldierly figure, all around. "We shall keep up the pursuit already inaugurated," he told me, "always following the hostiles and never giving them a respite. Thus we shall serve the double purpose of the campaign — to protect the settlements and to get hold of the hostiles. The pursuit will be maintained till we get them, dead or alive."

Within ten days of his arrival Miles has issued general

field orders distributing the Territory for thorough patrol. Signal detachments will be kept on the tops of the highest peaks to communicate the movements of the hostiles and infantry will be used between the camps in constant hunting through the mountains, occupying the passes, etc. A sufficient number of reliable Indians will be retained for trailers, cavalry will be used in light scouting, with a sufficient force always ready for instant, vigorous pursuit. To overcome the Apaches' advantage in relays of horses, commanders will dismount half their men and send the lightest and best riders in pursuit till all the animals are worn out. Thus the command should in forty-eight hours catch the hostiles or drive them one hundred fifty to two hundred miles, if the country is favorable for cavalry, and horses will be trained for the purpose. Commanding officers will thoroughly learn the topography of the section under their charge, and must continue the pursuit till they have captured the hostiles or until sure that a fresh command is on the trail. All camps and movements will be concealed as much as possible. To prevent the hostiles from getting ammunition, every cartridge will be accounted for, and all empty shells destroyed. Field reports are to be made thrice monthly.

When the grim, gray old soldier whom the Apaches also call Captain-with-the-Brown-Clothes left for the rest earned by thirty-three years of hard campaigning, the backbone of the Apache rebellion seemed broken, or at least badly sprained. Of the thirty-four men, eight well-grown boys and ninety-two women and children who left the reservation on the seventeenth of May, 1885, only twenty men and fourteen women were left upon the warpath. The rest were dead, or immured in a Florida prison. Geronimo and two or three others of the renegades were desperate and never would surrender, but it was extremely probable that Nachita and the rest would come in if properly approached. It was anticipated by all who best knew the circumstances and the Apache character that the hopelessly outlawed would bury themselves in the deepest recesses of Mexico and be heard of no more.

General Miles has, I am frank to say, done everything possible; but things in the Territory are a thousand-fold worse than when Crook left them. It is not Miles' fault, but a natural sequence. When Crook departed, the thirty-four hostiles were very sick, and asked nothing but to get away in the deepest recesses of old Mexico. The people on the reservation were quiet and contented, safe in the knowledge that Crook would stand between them and the white sharks who have already got the reservation cut down five times, and are trying to steal what is left. The renegades learned of the change in commanders about as soon as anybody, you may be sure. By what desert telegraph or journal of the winds they learn these things no man can say, yet the Indian is always to be relied upon to know all current matters of import to them. Their wholesome awe of the Gray Fox was gone. In his place they had a new foe, a general of whom they had never heard, and who had never seen Arizona. His friends and a vagabond press filled the air with prophecies of what was to be done. But the Chiricahua has a hideous humor of his own, and I can fancy the renegades smiling grimly as they set out to give the new administration a taste of "how it is yourself."

General Miles is a gallant and a brilliant soldier, an honorable man, an officer who is doing all that man can do. That his coming has made affairs in Arizona so much worse is his unearned misfortune, not his fault. He has the advantage always denied Crook of fair play and decency from the Territory, but he has the counterbalancing disadvantage of having neither prestige among the Apaches nor personal knowledge of their habits and their haunts. He is pushing the campaign with the utmost vigor, yet though he has about every able-bodied man in the department pressed into active service, all the while that indomitable little band of savages sweeps hither and yon like the eddying wind of their own deserts, laughing their pursuers to scorn. A body of troops by forced marches surrounds tonight the rocky fastnesses to which the renegades have been driven. Tomorrow morning a scouting party fifty miles away comes upon the smoking ruins of a lonely rancho whose sturdy owner lies there with a stake driven through his bowels and into the earth, while his wife, the victim of a thousand deaths, is stretched lifeless across her lifeless babe.

Such is Apache warfare. We have had but one "fair shake" with the hostiles in all these weeks. Captain Hatfield did come upon a little band of them, rout them and capture every whit of their camp outfit, even down to the frying pans. He pressed on in hot pursuit up a little cañon. Suddenly the bleak rocks spat fire and the sky rained lead. He had fairly walked into their trap. When the Apache gets you in that box there is but one thing to do, and that is to get out of it in the shortest way. To stay and fight is suicide — and Hatfield got out. He left upon the field all of the plunder just captured, and six of his men. Thus the fugitives recovered their own with interest. That also is Apache warfare.

It is now two months since I wrote the preceding pages. For these two months General Miles has had full control of the Department of Arizona, yet still the renegade has not been expurgated from the Apache page. On the contrary, he is more numerous and more fearful than before. He has shed more blood in these eight short weeks than in the three years preceding them, and has lost none of his own in the operation. Moreover, grave complications incident to the change of department commanders have arisen upon the reservation. Crook's name was not only a terror to the renegades, it was also a bulwark of restraint and protection to the eight thousand Apaches on the reservation. From every other hand they have been used to receiving outrage and imposition, and although I am far from apologizing for the hideous butcheries which they have committed, the Apaches have had many a strong excuse. The tale of the steals and swindles by which they have suffered would fill a volume. Crook, on the other hand, has no sickly sentimentalism, but he is a man. The foundation of his policy has been that the Apache, wild, bloodthirsty, and treacherous, was still a human being, that we must first whip him into submission and teach him to fear the results of disobedience, then we must win his confidence. It has been Crook's creed to make few promises, but to keep those few sacredly. He has given years of tedious work to instructing the Indian in the principles of civilization, self-support, and self-government. Visit the White Mountain reservation, inspect its farms, its great crops, its quiet farmers, who ten years ago were the most relentless butchers alive, and you will see something of what Crook has done aside from war. Now that he has left Arizona all Apachedom is apprehensive. The only barrier between the Apache and the white sharks of the Territory is gone. The government is no protection. It seems to the semi-civilized people a question either of going out again upon the warpath, or of submitting to outrages which their free blood will never brook. The whole reservation is unsettled. It is reiterated by the dispatches that scores of bucks are slipping away and joining the renegades. How true this is we are unable to tell yet, but it is undoubtedly imminent. I may remark in passing, however, that the long-current tales that Crook's recently discharged scouts have gone upon the war-path are and have been wilful lies. The scouts are not out.

There is certainly lots of fun in Arizona in consequence. The thirty-four renegades, three thousand soldiers, and thirty thousand Arizona liars are all doing their level best. The combination is a daisy. If there is a disgusted and surprised man in the United States at present, I fancy it is

Brigadier General Nelson A. Miles. He has fallen a victim to his friends. He is unlucky in having a lot of friends who are mouth-full in direct proportion to their ignorance of Arizona. They damned Crook by the acre, and bloviated that "if Miles was only there he'd show 'em how to fight Indians — he'd wipe out those few ragamuffins quicker than Sheol could scorch a feather." Well, Miles swallowed these jawy-ous friends, and came to believe himself that it wasn't much of a contract. He hasn't a bit of the braggart in him, but he remarked soon after getting to Bowie that he thought the Apaches could be whipped as easily as the Indians he had "downed" in the north, if one only went at it in the right way. The other day he admitted to a friend that he guessed he hadn't gone at it the right way. Moreover, it is my honest opinion that no man could have come in and quite filled Crook's place. What has happened has been only a natural sequence of the departure of a man who understood his job as does no other man in the country.

On June tenth, for example, a circumstantial account was telegraphed over the country that a huge band of hostiles had got clear over into People's Valley, near Prescott, three hundred and fifty miles from the scene of the real operations, and was slaying right and left. The Sheriff and a posse rushed out to see about it. They found, of course, there were no Indians and hadn't been any. A Mexican named Sieste Lavarice was mining in the mountains with a partner. They struck it rich. Lavarice wanted the whole bonanza, so he murdered his partner and went up and built fires on the mountans which would be taken for Indian signals. Then he came flying into town and reported that he had been chased by the hostiles, but managed to escape from them by night. Only strenuous efforts on the part of the Sheriff prevented a lynching when the truth was found out — and I hope they will succeed yet. This is one of the few cases where the truth has come out. Generally the lie is broadcasted and the exposure of it suppressed.

We have, also, the legitimate successors to the Tombstone Toughs — the alleged Rangers. You keep reading in the press how this or that company of Rangers has killed three or four renegades in some obscure place; but, strange to say, they never bring in a head to claim the handsome standing reward, and the hostiles still dodge from range to range, thumbing the tips of their noses. Anyone with a flair for mathematics will find that these jawbone Rangers have killed more Redskins than have ever been on the warpath. The beauty of the Arizona liar, however, is that his story is told by a facile telegraph to a world too far off to probe the truth. For instance, this morning's *Chronicle* has a column of rot telegraphed to it by its regulation liar at Tombstone. It says that when Geronimo left after the surrender, he had forty bucks and thirty-one women and children. As a matter of fact he had nineteen bucks, fourteen women and no children. The Tombstone truth-defacer knows that; but it is to his interest to make the thing as big as possible, so that more troops may be sent and he may get more coin for his dispatches.

I am the victim of a cruel fate. While we were all taking it easy at Fort Bowie, and the renegades had buried themselves in the bowels of Mexico, with no prospect of their emerging, the *Times* yanked me in to attend to some pressing work at home, but with the understanding that I was to go out again whenever anything lively developed upon the frontier. All of a sudden old Geronimo got on his ear again and began to paint the border red; but though I argued and orated, cajoled, damned and held on, I couldn't get away to see the fun. It's a hard dose. . . .

When I left Bowie, General Miles promised to notify me in time to join any expedition; and I have four very flattering telegrams to show how well he remembered his word. Then to be choked off and tied down to this dodgasted routine — isn't it enough to make anyone sick? The war is apt to last a year or two, however, and I hope that soon they will let me, once again, be off.